DISGRACELAND

DISGRACELAND

Musicians Getting Away with Murder and Behaving Very Badly

JAKE BRENNAN

GRAND CENTRAL
PUBLISHING

NEW YORK   BOSTON

Grand Central Publishing
Hachette Book Group
1290 Avenue of the Americas, New York, NY 10104
grandcentralpublishing.com
twitter.com/grandcentralpub

First Edition: October 2019

Grand Central Publishing is a division of Hachette Book Group, Inc. The Grand Central Publishing name and logo is a trademark of Hachette Book Group, Inc.

The publisher is not responsible for websites (or their content) that are not owned by the publisher.

The Hachette Speakers Bureau provides a wide range of authors for speaking events. To find out more, go to www.hachettespeakersbureau.com or call (866) 376-6591.

Illustrations by Matt Nelson.

Library of Congress Cataloging-in-Publication Data has been applied for.

ISBNs: 978-1-5387-3214-4 (hardcover), 978-1-5387-3213-7 (ebook)

Printed in the United States of America

LSC-C

10 9 8 7 6 5 4 3 2 1

For Johnny Angel.
Peace: I hope you found it, Brother.

CONTENTS

AUTHOR'S NOTE

Rock stars aren't like you and me. They act insane and have insane things happen to them. They are more like feral, narcissistic animals than functioning members of society, and this is in part what makes them so damn entertaining.

Journalists have dug deep into their pasts, their personal lives, and into the details surrounding not only their music but also their insane behavior, including the various crimes they've committed. Friends, lovers, and enemies have sold inside stories to the highest bidders, and some musicians have even penned their own auto-biographies in order to ensure the telling of *their own* history. The stories told in this book rely on all these types of different accounts to piece together a read that is hopefully as wild as the musicians covered within. This book is a stylized interpretation of these stories, melding true crime and transgressive fiction and aligning the musicians, the music they made, and the crimes they committed with the mythology that surrounds them.

I am indebted to the journalists, authors, and filmmakers who captured these stories first and got them down onto the record. I am also indebted to a small cast of co-conspirators who were more than generous with their time and offered me firsthand insight into some of the subjects covered herein. And I am indebted to the musicians who lived larger than life, proving themselves to be endlessly entertaining both on and off record.

To all of these folks, I say thank you.

Finally, a note about the victims: Each chapter of this book explores real people, not just human collateral damage strewn to the pay-no-mind list of history, products of the wild living done by the musicians; within these pages are dead spouses, relatives, bandmates, friends, and others who bear scars the likes of which we'll hopefully never have to carry. It would be irresponsible if I did not acknowledge them and include a legitimate note of sympathy for both the victims and for those who survived them. It is impossible to research these stories without feeling, at times, intense dread and astonishment at what the worst among us are capable of. I can only imagine that this darkness is but a small portion of the real-life pain felt by those affected by the rock 'n' roll animalism described herein.

DISGRACELAND

The beast in me
Is caged by frail and fragile bars
Restless by day
And by night rants and rages at the stars
God help the beast in me
—Nick Lowe by way of Johnny Cash

CHAPTER 1

FAT ELVIS

ELVIS COULDN'T GET THE BULLETS into the chamber: His fingers—swollen along with the rest of his body from a steady diet of greasy, fried Southern food and shaking from his daily narcotics cocktail of antidepressants and pain relievers, morphine, codeine, diazepam, and several other barbiturates—made it near impossible to concentrate, never mind possess the physical dexterity required to properly thread the barrel of his small snub-nosed revolver with the tiny .38 Special bullets.

Elvis could feel his temperature rising. He needed to get the gun loaded and get the shot off quick. Who knew how long it would be before the TV gods would deliver that handsome prick's two-faced mug to his television screen again. The sweat on his forehead puddled above his brow and dripped down the side of his bloated face. The Valium wasn't working and he needed another kind of release. He'd be up for hours unless he blew off some steam. Blasting Robert Goulet's shit-eating grin off his face with his .38-caliber Smith & Wesson—the one with the TCB logo and lightning bolt on the pistol grip—was likely the only chance left to lower his blood pressure tonight.

Goulet. Elvis hated him. Ever since Elvis shipped off to Germany and Goulet, back home, moved in on his girl. The bullet slid into the chamber just in time. THERE! Elvis's heart practically burst through his sternum at the sight of Goulet onscreen, appearing in an oft-run commercial for the 1977 television show *Police Story*. Elvis took aim. He held his fire as the commercial moved through B-plot characters before returning to Goulet.

Elvis didn't want to blow it. The shot had to be perfect. He needed to blast Goulet's face the very instant it filled the screen, otherwise his anxiety would remain pitched until morning. Sleep would never come, and he'd need to double down on amphetamines the next day to keep going. And besides, at this range, seated six feet away from the big RCA, there should only be one result: the kill shot.

THERE!!!!

Just then, Robert Goulet's impossibly tan skin and sapphire eyes covered the twenty-five-inch screen. Elvis squeezed his fat sausage finger against the trigger.

BOOM!

The sound of the .38's blast within the confines of Elvis's Graceland den was deafening but definitely worth it. Smoke rose out of the hole in his television where the smug face of Robert Goulet had been just one second earlier. Elvis sunk into himself with satisfaction. The feeling was almost postcoital, but despite the gratification, Elvis Presley, arguably the most popular entertainer in the world, had never felt more alone.

And alone Elvis kept the wolves at bay. Beasts that roamed freely throughout his drug-addled psyche, but one beast raged loudest: the thought of his twin brother, Jesse Garon Presley. Dead at birth. And Elvis's survivor's guilt was strong. As was his grief. The twin emotions gnawed away, creating a hole in him that no amount of drugs, women, food, money, fame or Robert Goulet–kill shots would fill.

Jesse Garon Presley, the brother was dead. God save Elvis Aaron Presley, the King.

But if someone was going to save Elvis Presley, they'd better do it fast. It was August 1977, and the King of Rock 'n' Roll was king in name only. He'd been dethroned long ago by the Beatles, who'd descended like their cousins, the locusts, laying waste to everything before them. Then by sympathetic satanists posing as harmless rolling stones but who tumbled him like dice off the charts. And most recently by lean anarchists armed with only three chords and the truth.

Gone were the heady and innocent days of newfound chart-topping success. His early triumph had been fueled by the accidental creation of a new type of earth-shattering music: rock 'n' roll.

Back then, Elvis's grip on the nation was firm. The world had never seen the likes of him before. He was the vessel for a new sound. He naturally infused white Southern country music into gutbucket black blues, and in doing so gave rock 'n' roll a level of relatability (and crossover commercial appeal) that was undeniable.

The world shook. Parents rattled. And Elvis rolled.

Rolled over the naysayers who miscast rock 'n' roll as a fad.

Rolled over the competition who misjudged him as a one-hit wonder.

And rolled over Beethoven, Tchaikovsky, and any and all traditional forms of music that got in his way. His first singles lit up the request lines of radio stations throughout the South, and Elvis

Fat Elvis shooting Robert Goulet.

quickly outgrew his little hometown record label. It was clear, almost from the jump, that Elvis Presley wasn't just a recording artist. He was a culture-shaping phenom on the make.

Back then in 1955, Elvis was lean himself. To most of America, with his long jet-black hair, acne-scarred cheeks, and slithering hips, he was just as alien looking as the punk rockers who now reviled him were in 1977.

In the here and now, holed up in his Graceland mansion den, aka the Jungle Room, Elvis Presley's kitschy, ostentatious, interior-designed man cave, with its animal prints, shag rug, and faux wood, he felt a million miles away from his humble beginnings despite the fact that he was only a fifteen-minute drive from 706 Union Avenue, the Memphis address of Sun Studio, where he'd gotten his start a couple decades earlier.

Elvis, bored, hit the intercom on the wall and called for Diamond Joe Esposito, an original member of the Memphis Mafia, his entourage, who—among other things—kept him entertained when the need for distraction took hold.

"Joe! Come on down to the den. I wanna shake it up tonight."

Within minutes Joe appeared.

"Joe, let's party, man. I'm bored. You see those girls outside the gates? Go bring 'em in the house."

"Elvis, there's about three hundred people outside the gates right now."

"I'm not talking about all those people. Just the girls. The older girls. We don't need none of that Jerry Lee nonsense. And tell the boys to get the bar stocked and I want some *I-talian* food. Call up Coletta's and get a bunch of them BBQ pizzas. Let's party, Joe."

Within no time there were roughly 150 women filling the walls of Graceland to accompany Elvis and the ten members of his Memphis Mafia entourage. Shooting fish in a barrel.

But Elvis wasn't interested in shooting fish. He sat in his chair and fingered his pistol. It gave Elvis a sense of security in these uncertain times. His career was at an all-time low. He wasn't yet broke, but his massive overhead was threatening to bust his bank. He hadn't had a top-ten hit since "Burnin' Love" five years earlier and hadn't had real critical acclaim since "Suspicious Minds" shot up the charts in 1969. But even then, nearly a decade before, he was still seen as past his prime. They wouldn't have referred to his 1968 NBC special as the "Comeback Special" if he'd been reliably ruling his kingdom the whole time. And now, he was a lifetime away from the supernova-star status of his early No. 1 hits "Heartbreak Hotel" and "Don't Be Cruel."

Truth be told, Elvis had been creatively spent for the better part of a decade. And physically, he was in the worst shape of his life. To make matters worse, Elvis's manager had him teed up to embark on a rigorous tour. It was a tour that he dreaded and was in no shape to do, physically or mentally.

Elvis couldn't help but wonder why he was in this mess. How did it get to this point? Lonely, running out of bread, and out of shape. He was only forty-two years old. And only a couple decades removed from being the undisputed King of Rock 'n' Roll. The more he thought about it, the more he came back to blaming the one person he could never confront head-on. His manager, the Colonel. Colonel Tom Parker.

Colonel Tom Parker had been an outsized figure in Elvis Presley's life ever since 1955, just as Elvis's first singles started to crack the charts. The Colonel was a talent manager and not actually a colonel. He was born Andreas Cornelis van Kuijk, was from Breda, Holland, and was in reality an illegal immigrant who'd hoodwinked Jimmie Davis, the Louisiana governor and a one-time country star himself, to bestow upon him the honorary title of Colonel because he thought it made him seem more American.

A new identity was a necessity for the Colonel. His days in Holland have been shaded by time but one theory goes that young Andreas Cornelis van Kuijk left Holland for the United States to escape a murder rap. Once in the States, he'd grifted his way through the Depression, making ends meet through a series of short cons until eventually finding work on the carnival circuit as a carny barker. It was there, in the carnival, where the wannabe Colonel would form his business philosophy: Entertainers, be it an elephant in a ring, a monkey in a cage, a lady with a beard, or a singer with a song, they were all the same. They weren't artists, they were *attractions*.

Once the United States got off the skids and Americans started spending money on entertainment again, Andreas, in the spirit of most hardworking immigrants before him, assimilated and began climbing the social ladder through hard work. The carnival was out. There was money to be made in the devil's workshop, aka the music industry. So he began hustling tickets and dates for country music singers Minnie Pearl and Eddy Arnold, and he eventually built up enough clout to con Governor Davis into giving him that new handle. Now that he was "officially" the Colonel, he could fully become the prototype of the big barrel-bellied, cigar-chomping American music businessman. Colonel Tom Parker was poised to deliver a star attraction to the masses. All he needed was to find that attraction.

Elvis couldn't remember exactly when he first met Colonel Tom Parker. When he thought back to those early days, the scene that always played out in his head was the day he signed his management contract with the Colonel. His mama's kitchen was small to begin with but was made smaller by the presence of Parker and his business partner, the country singer Hank Snow, whom Elvis's parents admired deeply.

Everybody in the room had a different idea of what was happening.

Elvis's parents believed their son was signing a management contract with Hank Snow, one of the most respected names in the entertainment business at the time. And that Colonel Tom Parker, who they didn't really care for personally but believed brought some business acumen to the table, was a necessary evil. He was Snow's partner, so he couldn't be all bad.

Hank Snow believed that he was cosigning a personal management contract to manage the brightest young star in America.

And young Elvis, ever the pleaser, believed he was making everybody happy, particularly his mama, and that he was going to be a big star.

But like most confidence men, Colonel Parker believed only in the card up his sleeve, which right now was the actual contract that everyone was signing. Grifter that he was, the Colonel knew where he was vulnerable. He could sense the Presleys' distrust in him, and he knew that they trusted his partner, Hank. So Hank was in the room. But he wouldn't be for long. The contract was drafted exclusively to be between the Colonel and Elvis. Soon after the signing, Hank Snow would ask the Colonel about the status of his contract and the Colonel would reply, "You don't have any contract with Elvis Presley. Elvis is signed exclusively to the Colonel." Hank Snow was out.

Despite this messiness, Elvis was right about one thing—he was going to be a big star. But his mother's happiness would not last. After the signing that day, after the room cleared out and Hank headed out to the front lawn to speak with Vernon, Elvis's dad,

Elvis saw the Colonel speaking to his mother in the kitchen, in private and in hushed tones. And there was no mistaking the look on his mother's face: stone-cold fear.

Colonel Tom Parker was evil. If, as the Good Book says, being creative brings you closer to God—who in his infinite artistry created all living things in his own image—then someone who crushes creativity in favor of profit can be seen as the opposite of God, or the opposite of good.

And he has filled him with the Spirit of God—and with all kinds of skills—to make artistic designs for work.

—Exodus 35:31

The Colonel couldn't give a shit about "artistic designs for work." He didn't care about blues or country music or Elvis's favorite form of music, gospel.

Elvis had that indefinable "it," and the Colonel knew that people would travel far and wide and empty their pockets to see it. Elvis was an attraction: a step removed from a novelty.

Elvis's heart might have been with the Lord's gospel music, but his true religion was rock 'n' roll. And the Colonel, like most sane thinking adults back in 1955, thought rock 'n' roll was merely a fad that would burn out quick, so he'd better do what needed doing: Milk this golden cow and fast. He moved swiftly to extract Elvis from his contract with Sun Records and moved him over to RCA, one of the powerhouse record labels of the 1950s music industry.

And Elvis didn't disappoint. Under this brighter spotlight, Elvis recorded magnificent music. His first single for RCA, "Heartbreak Hotel," quickly shot up to No. 1 on the pop chart and would ultimately go platinum twice over. "Blue Suede Shoes," a single released shortly after, was no less a masterpiece. Both RCA releases

Colonel Tom Parker, carny-barking soul sucker.

somehow upgraded the raw style Elvis displayed on Sun Records but lost none of the energy.

The Colonel then arranged for Elvis to perform live on national television on the Dorsey Brothers' *Stage Show*, *The Milton Berle Show*, and *The Steve Allen Show*. He then negotiated three coveted and high-paying appearances on *The Ed Sullivan Show*, and when they aired? America freaked…the fuck…out.

The puppy dog eyes. The pouty lips and the polite Southern drawl, the long sideburns. All that energy, all that charm, and those swiveling hips. Americans couldn't help but wonder: With all that going for him on the outside, what had God bestowed upon him under those trousers?

Having quickly conquered radio and television, the Colonel set his sights on Hollywood and began to negotiate a series of film deals for Elvis that would feature him in starring roles and also serve as vehicles to promote music recorded for the films' soundtracks.

This was a distillation of the Colonel's carny philosophy for the modern era. The Colonel made the calculated decision to hold Elvis back from his fans: to give them glimpses of his star attraction only through carefully planned film releases to maximize ticket sales.

When Uncle Sam came calling and drafted the biggest star in the land at the height of his popularity? The Colonel saw it as a blessing. Send Elvis off to Germany and keep the fans starving for more. After all, he had enough material lying around from the RCA sessions to release Elvis singles in dribs and drabs to keep 'em hooked until Elvis's triumphant return.

And that was what happened. By the time his Army stint ended, Elvis came back bigger than ever. He appeared on television with Frank Sinatra on *The Frank Sinatra Timex Special* and camped it up. America loved it. Their two biggest pop stars; one representing the comfort of the past and one the promise of the future.

But Elvis would find that his future would quickly go from white-hot heat to what-the-fuck-am-I-doing-with-my-career in a matter of a few short years.

With his star attraction back Stateside, the Colonel moved quickly to tighten the reins. Elvis was eager to record new material, and he did. *Elvis Is Back!*—with excellent material by Jerry Leiber, Mike Stoller, Lowell Fulson, and Otis Blackwell—was a critical and commercial success and one that Elvis himself was pleased with. However, his first film, *G.I. Blues*, was another story. Elvis didn't want to do the movie. He knew the plot was bunk. However, the bigger sin was the soundtrack. The material simply did not compare to the music Elvis had been recording to that point, and that had everything to do with the songwriters. The Colonel was consolidating control, and top songwriters like Leiber and Stoller sought and received a share of the songwriting profits for their talents. Because of this, they were jettisoned for backbenchers who didn't have any business writing material for one of the biggest performers in the world. The Colonel would have it no other way because Elvis would retain as much of the profit as possible. Leiber and Stoller weren't going to be swindled out of their rightful share of the publishing profits, so the Colonel—with zero regard for the quality of the material his artist would be staking his soul on—told Leiber and Stoller to fuck off.

And Elvis went along with it.

From a commercial standpoint it didn't matter. The soundtrack sold more copies than *Elvis Is Back!* It skyrocketed to the top of the charts on the success of the *G.I. Blues* film, which, despite its cheese factor, was a smash. It turns out 50 million Elvis fans *can* be wrong, because the movie is indeed bunk. Elvis knew it, but he went along with it.

The Colonel promised him that by giving the studio what they wanted—the campy *G.I. Blues* flick—Elvis would be able to get back to what he cared about: becoming the next James Dean or Marlon Brando. A serious actor. A path he'd begun with *Loving You* and *King Creole*, among the first films he'd made before entering the Army.

And the manager kept his promise. After *G.I. Blues*, Elvis delivered one of the most creatively rewarding and critically received performances of his career in the Western *Flaming Star*. But after that concession, the Colonel laid down the lash on his young thoroughbred, pressuring him to bang out film after film after film with little to no regard for quality of script or production. Most of the films Elvis would go on to star in throughout the remainder of the '60s would all be marred by inadequate production budgets ("The less you spend, the more you make!") and less than stellar material ("We have Elvis Presley, the biggest star in the world—who needs a script?!") and result in a long parade of poor artistic output at the box office.

The exception was *Viva Las Vegas*, in which he starred opposite Ann-Margret. The chemistry between them was undeniable. Elvis, one of the most charismatic performers of all time, was now sharing the screen with a five-alarm smoke show, and the results were *electric*. Watching the two together, you couldn't take your eyes off Ann-Margret. She nearly upstaged the king. The big screen could hardly contain the double dose of sex appeal. Audiences begged for more.

Now Elvis could get into *this*. Ann was fun. And suddenly the moviemaking business wasn't a drag. Not only was Elvis happy, the studio was happy, having benefited from one of the highest-grossing films of 1964. Talks of future box office pairings were in the air. However, the Colonel would have none of it. He wasn't going to risk Elvis's star being outshined again by Ann-Margret's blinding sex appeal.

And Elvis went along with it.

So it was right back to whatever lot or location where the next reel of bad film was being shot. This work schedule had the added disadvantage of preventing Elvis from performing live, which he was keen on doing since he'd debuted his studio band live at a benefit in Honolulu while shooting the film *Blue Hawaii*. The band tore it up, and Elvis was excited to do more shows, but the Colonel wasn't buying it. Why spend money flying a band around the country to reach fans when the Colonel could, for a bigger profit, throw Elvis up on movie screens across the country and reach more people for less investment?

And Elvis went along with it.

He was contractually obligated to make three films a year: A tremendous schedule to keep up with, and one that all but ensured Elvis would not have the time or the creative juice to continue to make studio albums, let alone long-playing artistic statements like the Beatles and the Rolling Stones were making. No, the Colonel assured him, the soundtrack albums from the movies were all the fans needed.

And Elvis went along with it.

But that material was shit and Elvis knew it. His ear for music that suited his voice, that he *knew* he could nail emotionally and deliver straight to the hearts of his audience, was unmatched. The singles "Love Me Tender," "Don't Be Cruel," "Jailhouse Rock," "Peace in the Valley," and "All Shook Up" were not just stone-cold hits, they were artistic statements on par with anything released before, during, or since. Elvis knew this was where the juice was. He knew that his future as an artist wasn't in camp, moneymaking movies but in making serious records—serious artistic statements. But again, the Colonel would have none of it. There was more money to be made in the studio contract that awaited them around the bend, and so:

Elvis went along with it.

Whenever the creative ran up against the carny, the carnival mentality won out.

Whatever you do, work at it with all your heart, as working for the Lord, not for human masters.

—Colossians 3:23

The toll that making movies took on Elvis was intense. He was worked like a dog. Scratch that—he was worked like a circus animal. To keep up the pace, Elvis turned to pills. Speed to keep up with the daily schedule. Sleeping pills to allow him to crash. And the result of the pill popping, the hard work, and the knowledge that the movies and music he was making was crap? Depression. It was all deeply depressing for Elvis. And with depression came that old fear.

The fear that he was unworthy. The fear that this dissatisfaction was something he deserved. In those deep, dark moments, late at night on set. His mind caught between the speed and the sleeping pills, his head wired and heavy on his pillow, Elvis couldn't shake the thought of his brother, Jesse. In Elvis's mind, his brother who died at birth was a purer version of himself, an aspirational, angelic, and judgmental avatar for all the things he longed to be but never became. Jesse's death was an ever-present reminder of how he had fallen short in his own life. He had survived the trauma of a deadly childbirth and the dirt-floor poverty of his youth to become the biggest star the world had ever seen—and for what? To line some fat-cat, cigar-chewing, carny barker's pockets? To not fully realize his God-given talent?

Elvis felt like a traitor. He believed he was betraying the Lord by not fully harnessing the gift the Creator had bestowed upon him and no one else. He had squandered the promise of his one and only trip through this mortal coil, a trip that was denied his brother. Maybe it should have been him who died at birth. Maybe Jesse would have handled it differently.

> Do not neglect your gift, which was given you through prophesy.
>
> —1 Timothy 4:14

The guilt, the grief, the shame, it was gnawing. The hole in him grew. So Elvis fed it. He stuffed it full of pills. He ate with the appetite of a small gospel congregation, filling his belly daily with the rich, cholesterol-filled, unhealthy Southern fried cuisine he'd grown up on. And he tried plugging the hole with a long string of women, who, no matter how beautiful or understanding, always came up short of satisfying him in the end.

And tonight in the Jungle Room, it was nothing new. After the meatloaf sandwich he'd had for dinner, Elvis gorged on BBQ pizza. He'd shot out Robert Goulet on the television. The Demerol he'd taken afterward to cool out before bed had his head spinning. His brain hurt. He was second-guessing his decision to throw a party. It was late. Real late. And he could hear sirens outside the gates of Graceland. Must've had something to do with the crash he'd heard earlier. He tried blocking it all out. Grabbed another handful of pills and threw them to the back of his throat. The drugs did little.

And tonight, along with being haunted by his dead brother, Elvis couldn't shake the thought of the Colonel. Elvis was bent on ending things. Firing the Colonel once and for all and getting on with his career. But deep down, Elvis knew he'd wake up in the morning and do nothing.

Despite the fact that most, if not all of the soul-crushing, profit-maximizing career missteps he'd made were at the Colonel's insistence. Despite the fact that the Colonel took 50 percent—*50 percent!!!!*—of his earnings, as opposed to the customary 15 percent management fee. Despite the fact that the Colonel was universally loathed by most everyone who came in contact with him. Despite all of this, Elvis couldn't shake him.

Because Elvis feared the Colonel knew the truth. The *truth* about his brother.

CHAPTER 2

JERRY LEE LEWIS

"KILLER." THE VOICE WAS STERN but deferential. "The hell you doing out here so late? You fucked your Lincoln up gooood this time. The hell you doing?"

The hood of the Lincoln was a semi-accordion-shaped mess, wedged hard into Graceland's front gate. Steam rising off the engine. Headlights shining aimlessly over Elvis Presley's front lawn. The Lincoln's engine was dead, but Webb Pierce's voice sounded very much alive warbling out of the speakers and into the misty Memphis morning air: "Thaaiir…staaands tha glass…"

"Killer! Jerry Lee!!! Come on, now. Wake up. The hell you doing here anyway?"

Slowly, the Killer picked his head up off the steering wheel and twisted it in the direction of the Memphis cop silhouetted through the driver's side window. His eyes were barely slits. His hair was a tousled blond halo of snakes. His breath was worthy of a walk-on role in a horror movie, and his voice was drowning in Talwin and cheap champagne, making his words all the more menacing as he whispered, "I'm here to assassinate the King."

The King. Fuck that. Elvis was a punk. Jerry Lee Lewis was the real king of rock 'n' roll. It said so right there on his new hunting knife. The one he planned on using to stick fat Elvis with, that past-his-prime, pill-popping poser. Fuck the King. Long live the Killer.

People started calling Jerry Lee Lewis "the Killer" back when he was in middle school. Long before he shot his bass player in the chest with a .357 Magnum. Long before he tried to blast Chuck Berry away with a shotgun. Long before he shot so much speed into his stomach that he almost killed *himself.* And of course, long before his newlywed beauty queen wife wound up dead in the guest bedroom of their house.

But back before all *that*, back in the '50s, the Killer was giving the King a serious run for the Colonel's money. It's hard to believe now but back in the day, the question of who was going to wear rock 'n' roll's crown was wide open. Elvis Presley was heading off to boot camp and Jerry Lee Lewis was heading up the charts.

In the span of nine months—from April 1957 to January 1958—Jerry Lee Lewis released three mega singles, each one more suggestive than the next. Jerry Lee's delivery pushed the young genre of rock 'n' roll closer to the edge than Elvis had with his swinging hips: "Whole Lotta Shakin' Going On," "Great Balls of Fire," and "Breathless" are all classics of the rock 'n' roll canon.

Both rockers captivated bobby-soxers and grease monkeys everywhere with their methods for stirring heretofore unmentionable teenage desires; Elvis was sex incarnate. Jerry Lee was violence incarnate. Elvis, dark and brooding. Jerry Lee, white lightning in flesh and in blood.

Jerry Lee's live shows were legend. The way he performed—primal energy coursing through his core and radiating to every fiber of his body, from his shaking legs to the wild hurricane of hair on top of his head—hadn't been seen before in popular music, or anywhere else. He rattled with violence and excitement as he bent his six-hundred-pound piano to his will while his googly eyes scanned the room for nonbelievers, of which there were none.

Jerry Lee's madman reputation preceded him. Rumors circulated that he was possessed. That he had been touched by the devil. Jerry Lee himself believed these rumors. How else could you account for his outsized talent? Jerry Lee liked to play, but it wasn't like he practiced more than other musicians as a child. He didn't take lessons. Couldn't read music. Wasn't particularly disciplined in any way, shape, or form. He was just a natural. When he sat down at the piano, pounded the keys with his long, spidery fingers, and banged his head and hair down toward the keyboard in time with the rhythm he kept with his left hand, the music just sort of happened. It wasn't this big thought-out thing. It just was. To Jerry Lee, his talent was a divine mystery. That was something he came to believe as a young boy, sitting in his pew in the Pentecostal church in his hometown of Ferriday, Louisiana.

Jerry Lee's talent certainly wasn't the Lord's work. No, the Lord's work was the domain of his first cousin, televangelist Jimmy Swaggart. In the South where Jerry Lee and Jimmy were from, cousin Jimmy was a star in his own right and had thus far stayed on the right side of Satan, while Jerry Lee did the devil's dirty work, singing secular songs about teenage lust. And if his musical ability couldn't be attributed to the good Lord above, then there was only one other option. And it scared the hell out of him. Was he, as they whispered, "touched"? "Possessed"? The thought kept him up at night and it woke him up in the morning, so he drowned his fear in alcohol and chased it away with speed.

At the end of the day, what did it really matter? Whatever Jerry Lee Lewis was doing, it was working. His televangelist cousin, in the South at least, may have been more famous than him, but Jerry Lee Lewis was a hellhound on Elvis Presley's tail.

Jerry Lee despised most of his fellow first-generation rock 'n' rollers. Particularly Elvis. Truly hated him. He thought—no, he *knew* in his bones that Elvis was a hack and that he couldn't hold a candle to real musical originators like himself, or Hank Williams or Al Jolson. As far as Jerry Lee was concerned, Colonel Tom Parker bet on the wrong horse. Just as well. Jerry Lee didn't need the Colonel. Especially not if he was taking a 50 percent management fee. "Shit," Jerry Lee wondered, "how stupid *is* Elvis?"

Later in his career, when the press asked Jerry Lee about Elvis Presley's influence on American culture, Jerry Lee flatly said, "Elvis this, Elvis that. What the shit did Elvis ever do except take dope that I couldn't get ahold of?" But when all was said and done, Elvis was the King: He wore the crown that Jerry Lee thought was rightfully his. At least it was his before that mess over in England back in the 1950s.

If you know two things about Jerry Lee Lewis, they are likely the piano lick to "Great Balls of Fire" and that he married his thirteen-year-old cousin, Myra Gayle Brown. Technically, Myra was Jerry Lee's first cousin once removed—she was the daughter of another first cousin (and Jerry Lee's bass player) J. W. Brown—but no matter how you try to justify it, she was just thirteen. And Jerry Lee was also still married to his second wife. He was twenty-two and *already* on wife number three, who was barely a teenager. It was reported that when Myra moved in with the Killer, she didn't have much in the way of proper luggage, so she resorted to the biggest vessel she could find: a dollhouse.

When news of Jerry Lee's child bride was made public, it ruined him. He had arrived in England for a much heralded tour in 1958. He had gotten there *before* Elvis, who was serving in the Army at the time. And just as Jerry Lee was positioned to snatch that King of Rock 'n' Roll crown from Elvis's flattopped head, a reporter asked about the girl by his side. He lied and boosted her age by two years, telling the press that she was fifteen, but he told the truth that she was his wife.

The press lost its collective mind. To the British, marrying your cousin? Marrying a fifteen-year-old? It was barbaric. Uncivilized. Unimaginable. And so very scandalous. The tabloids nearly ran out of ink. Suddenly it all made sense! Jerry Lee's hits—"Whole Lotta Shakin' Goin' On," "Great Balls of Fire," and especially "High School Confidential"—were all viewed through the prism of his newly discovered pedophilic lifestyle.

The press, justifiably, crucified Jerry Lee both in the UK and back home in the States. In a heartbeat, he went from making $10,000 a night to being kicked out of the country, blacklisted on the radio back home, and stringing together one-nighters for a couple hundred bucks here and there.

His reputation never really recovered, but by the early '70s, Jerry Lee did regain his fame *and* his fortune. He was conquering the charts again. This time as a country singer, with hit after hit after hit. Between 1968 and 1977, Jerry Lee had seventeen top-ten hits on the Billboard Country charts. It wasn't the pre—"I married my teenage cousin" international sensation status he'd had at the start of his career, but it was a *hugely* popular run: By late '70s–early '80s standards, Jerry Lee Lewis was once again a household name.

Success or lack of success, it didn't matter. Jerry Lee's demons were still there. He did his best to outrun them. Fueled by speed, alcohol, and a burning desire to never again lose the fame and fortune he'd now rediscovered, Jerry Lee crisscrossed the United States and Europe, playing hundreds of shows a year. Suddenly, money wasn't a problem anymore, at least if he could keep his fourth wife, Jaren, out of his pocket, and the IRS off his back.

But then in 1981, all of that speed he'd been taking caught up to him, and his stomach nearly exploded. The doctors gave him no better than even odds that he'd live. Friends like Johnny Cash and Elizabeth Taylor came by the hospital to say their farewells. But miraculously, he got better, and in April 1982, looking beaten up and worse for wear, he appeared on HBO, in a special celebrating *25 Years of Jerry Lee Lewis*.

"They call me the Killer," he told the audience, "but the only thing I ever killed in my life was possibly myself."

Maybe that was true. But the coming years would be full of death and mayhem.

In 1979, the tax men raided Jerry Lee Lewis's Nesbit, Mississippi, home. The one that locals were now commonly referring to as "Disgraceland" because of the way Jerry Lee's life—at least in the public's estimation—stood in contrast to the life of their hero, Elvis Presley. Not surprisingly, the raid of Disgraceland turned up cocaine and marijuana. Then in 1984, the IRS were back, bringing to court a case against Jerry Lee for tax evasion from 1975 to 1980. Jerry Lee was acquitted of the tax evasion charge, but he still had to pay back taxes.

And then more trouble: A looming divorce settlement from Jaren threatened to bankrupt Jerry Lee yet again. But as Jerry

Lee's "luck" would have it, Jaren mysteriously turned up dead in a friend's swimming pool. There were no witnesses. The official ruling? An accident.

For Jerry Lee, it was no doubt a convenient accident. Because with Jaren out of the picture, he wouldn't be on the hook for the expensive divorce settlement she was seeking.

A year after Jaren's death—almost to the day—the Killer took bride number five, Shawn Michelle Stevens, a cocktail waitress from Michigan nearly half his age. On June 7, 1983, on a tree-shaded patio on Jerry Lee's eighty-acre estate—the one with the piano-shaped pool out back—they were married: Jerry Lee wore a white tux, Shawn a white dress, of course, and a fat $7,000 wedding ring. The *National Enquirer* was on hand to shoot the photos. The new couple beamed.

But the light in Shawn's eyes wouldn't last. Less than three months later, Shawn was dead. The official cause of death, like Jerry Lee's wife before her: an accident.

But unlike Jaren's death, Shawn's attracted some attention: Police reports had gone missing, and a whole bunch of questionable evidence was uncovered at the scene. When the EMTs turned up at Jerry Lee's house in response to his 911 call, they found Shawn's body with blood under her fingernails and bruises on her body and, perhaps most suspicious, scrapes on Jerry Lee's hands.

The nearby Memphis newspaper, forever friendly to their local star, rolled over. But in Detroit—near where Shawn's parents lived—reporters were intrigued for obvious reasons: A local girl married a genuine celebrity and was found dead, less than three months after the wedding and only twelve months after his previous wife died under circumstances that could only generously be called "mysterious." The Detroit press smelled a rat. Something was up, so they dug in. And they uncovered details that the local Memphis press and authorities would have preferred remained buried. Those details simply didn't add up. To some, the death of Mrs. Jerry Lee Lewis was starting to look like a cover-up, and not a very good one.

And to think, just seventy-seven days earlier, Shawn Stevens Lewis was happily married. To a bona fide celebrity, to boot! Sure, he was a raging speed freak, an alcoholic, paranoid enough to sleep with a loaded pistol under his pillow, but he was a celebrity nonetheless. Marital bliss soon gave way to the reality of living with a spoiled, narcissistic, drug- and alcohol-addled rock star who was used to getting his way all the time and beholden to absolutely nobody.

Shawn got hip quick: Jerry Lee liked to drink. A lot.

Rule no. 1: Let him.

Jerry Lee's stomach hurt. A lot.

Rule no. 2: Get used to him shooting Talwin straight into his belly with that big ugly needle.

Jerry Lee liked attention from the ladies.

Rule no. 3: Don't give a fucking inch! Jerry Lee is YOUR man. Grab that needy slut by the hair and tell her to fuck right off back to the dirt-floor shack her white trash mama failed to do her the favor of miscarrying in, and get back to the business of being the one and only Mrs. Jerry Lee Fucking Lewis. Jerry Lee is like a needy puppy, and he *needs* to be reminded of who his woman is.

And like most needy men, Jerry Lee was jealous. Really jealous, even though his eyes wandered and the eyes of women everywhere wandered right back. Not only was Shawn determined to not give an inch, she also wasn't afraid to let her man know she was no sucker. Confidentially, a high school crush was waiting for her back in Michigan should things with Jerry Lee not work out. Eventually,

The Killer, Jerry Lee Lewis.

Shawn revealed to Jerry Lee that she had an exit strategy and threatened to leave. *That* did not please the Killer. Not at all.

"You're my wife," he said. "I'll kill you before you leave me."

It wasn't long before Shawn also learned that Jerry Lee liked group sex. Why settle for one woman when a romp with two or three would be even better? Shawn was cool, but a swinger she was not, especially not with her younger sister, Shelley. Jerry Lee had been trying to maneuver Shelley during one of her visits to the newlywed couple. When Shelley batted away Jerry Lee's advances, his reaction was something between petulance and rage. Banging his fist into a counter, he screamed at her.

"You scared of me? You should be. Why do you think they call me the Killer? How'd I get that name, huh?" And then, to seal the point, he slapped Shelley hard across her face.

Shawn was scared. She needed to get out or she was likely to wind up beaten or, worse, dead.

And that was what happened.

Shortly after the incident with Jerry Lee and her sister, Shawn Stevens Lewis was found dead in their home.

For the local EMTs who took the call, there was nothing out of the ordinary about heading over to Jerry Lee's to provide medical assistance to some passed-out reveler. It was part of the gig. Finding a dead body, though? That was something new.

Upon arrival, the EMTs were confused. Jerry Lee was nowhere to be found—which was odd, considering Jerry Lee had called in the dead body. The perplexities didn't end there. Strangely, to the EMTs, the body seemed to be *placed* on the fully made bed in the couple's *guest room* as opposed to being in their bedroom, which was where one would naturally expect a newlywed couple to sleep at night. The EMTs checked for vitals while Lottie Jackson, Jerry Lee's caretaker of more than a decade, knocked on his bedroom door. Within seconds, the Killer emerged.

Immediately, the EMTs noticed the bright red scratches on the back of Jerry Lee's hand. They looked like the kind of scratches a pet cat would make. Except Jerry Lee didn't own a cat. Blood was also visible on Jerry Lee's robe. And on his slippers. There was a pile of bloody clothes in the bathroom. A rivulet of blood on a door. More blood on the carpet. Broken glass was scattered across the floor throughout the house, among what appeared to be the remnants of a small personal pill pharmacy and at least one hypodermic syringe. *What the hell happened?*

There was also blood on Shawn's dead hand. In her hair. On her clothes. And on a bra that was in another room. There was dirt all over her body. Bruises on her arms. On her hip. Her fingernails were broken, and they had something that looked a lot like blood under-neath. Freaked out, the EMTs quietly went about their business. With a mountain of sketchy physical evidence, a woman lying dead on top of a neatly made bed that wasn't hers, and a drug-addled rock star, they were far out of their depth.

This scene just didn't make sense. And it made even less sense that said evidence wouldn't be reported. At least not until *after* the grand jury convened, ensuring, of course, that the grand jury would find no indication of foul play.

Jerry Lee Lewis had DeSoto County, Mississippi, wound tightly around his finger. He had to. He couldn't live the way he lived—raising hell, doing whatever the hell he pleased, whenever the hell he damned well wanted and to whomever he crossed paths

Jerry Lee Lewis shooting speed straight into his belly.

with—without first making friends with the county cops and politicians.

Elvis the King's fiefdom was Memphis—up the road a piece—so Jerry Lee's kingdom became DeSoto. When DeSoto County law officials needed him, Jerry Lee showed up with his fat rock star wallet. He made the appropriate campaign contributions to the appropriate men who made sure that DeSoto County remained an appropriate place to fear God in, and to raise your children up right in. Jerry Lee was one of their own. So when Jerry Lee fucked up, they didn't arrest him: They made sure the mess went away. Who needed it, anyway? The resulting press and the headache of having to type up a report and to go to court, and for what? So the judge could send Jerry Lee straight back to the bar with a slap on the wrist and a token fine? Nah. Better to just solve the problem on the spot. Send Jerry Lee home. Get him to sleep it off. He'd remember who his friends were by morning and likely drop a bottle of Chivas off at the station as a thank-you.

So, on the night before Shawn's death, when Jerry Lee drove his car off the road and into a ditch, DeSoto County deputies simply had his car towed and gave him a ride home. They didn't even test him for intoxication. Why bother? Jerry Lee was clearly wasted. The sheriff's department didn't trouble themselves recording the incident, either. County dispatcher John Crawford said at the time, "I knew not to log it or nothing. When I heard it was Jerry Lee Lewis, I knew it was just a community service."

And it was in this culture that the investigation of Jerry Lee's newest dead wife was to take place.

The case never stood a chance. When state investigators arrived at the scene of the crime on the morning Shawn was found dead, DeSoto County officials were already muddling through the house and mucking up the crime scene. State investigators later reported that Jerry Lee had been secluded in his den—alone—with DeSoto County deputy sheriff Jack McCauley for more than an hour by the time they arrived.

When they emerged from that conversation, state investigators were informed that the decision had *already* been made by *county* investigators—unilaterally—to use a *private* medical examiner instead of a public one.

This meant that DeSoto County would control the flow of information surrounding the death of Shawn Lewis. Apparently the state investigators were fine with this. Less work.

The county, DeSoto County, Jerry Lee Lewis's county, would handle the medical examination and ensure that any and all sordid details from Shawn's death would never be placed in the public record. They'd be buried so deep they'd never see the light of day.

However, to Danny Phillips, the young funeral director who received Shawn's body, the physical evidence reeked of foul play, and he was either too stupid or too principled to clam up about it. Phillips said at the time, "I'd never say Jerry Lee killed that girl...but I'd like to see it investigated. To me, I just can't believe that girl just got to that bed and lay down and died. You just can't make me believe it."

Phillips was particularly perplexed by his finding of what he thought to be a puncture wound caused by a hypodermic needle on Shawn's right arm. The same type of needle found at Jerry Lee's house that day.

Despite the needle.

Despite the puncture wound in Shawn's arm.

Despite the overwhelming amount of physical evidence on the scene.

The bruises on her body.

The dirt on her body.

The blood under her fingernails.

The defensive-looking scratches on Jerry Lee's hand.

The broken shards of glass scattered throughout the house.

And despite the fact that with all this mayhem, county investigators reached the hard-to-believe conclusion that Shawn crawled up onto a perfectly made bed to go to sleep in a bedroom that wasn't hers, lay down, closed her eyes, and died peacefully.

Despite all of this, local DeSoto County authorities officially ruled the death an accident without even conducting a full investigation.

The private medical examiner quickly declared "no foul play," and the body was shipped out of the lab within hours to be embalmed.

DeSoto County sheriff Dink Sowell explained away the crime scene evidence at Jerry Lee's place, stating that the blood was from Jerry Lee cutting his finger on a glass. He made no mention of the countless shards of broken glass throughout the house, or of the scratches on Jerry Lee's hand, or of the blood under Shawn's fingernails. Authorities described Shawn's bruises as "superficial."

Sheriff Sowell claimed there were "no marks of any violence" and no indication of anyone being attacked.

County attorney Bill Ballard declared it a "complete and thorough" investigation despite the fact that the lab tests to determine whose blood was on the scene weren't yet completed.

Putting aside the physical evidence, investigators didn't seem to care that three nights before Shawn's death, Jerry Lee took two women home for sex with him and Shawn. At some point things got scary, and the two women were spooked enough to run out of the house and to frantically beg Jerry Lee's neighbors for a ride out of there. Did Shawn try to escape, too? This anecdotal detail was never given to the grand jury.

The case never stood a chance. Which is maddening, given that Shawn made two calls the night before her death. The first was made late to her mom. Shawn told her she was thinking of leaving Jerry Lee but that he wouldn't let her. Shawn's mom thought she was upset and that by morning it would all blow over. They made plans to talk later and hung up.

Then Shawn made a second call. This one wasn't to family, but to the sister of her hometown sweetheart, Scott. He was the one Shawn mentioned to Jerry Lee during their argument over the countless women threatening their relationship. Shawn wanted to know if Scott still loved her. She was planning her exit, and they agreed that Scott's sister would come for her later that month. Then—in midsentence—the phone went dead.

On the day they found Shawn dead, while the local cops and state investigators got down to the business of securing the scene and coming up with their own interpretations of what the words *complete* and *thorough* meant, Jerry Lee decamped fifteen miles north to the home of his manager, J.W. Whitten. Reporters were ringing the phone off the hook. Looking for a comment from the Killer about his newest dead wife to run in their evening editions: "So tragic…how was he able to stand the strain?" that sort of thing. But J.W.—ever Jerry Lee's keeper—made it clear that the Killer would not be able to come to the phone. He was supposedly "in shock" and "heavily sedated."

Jerry Lee could feel the heat on the back of his neck. The

sweat, beading off his forehead, stung his already bloodshot eyes. He needed to get high. And quick. Or who knew what he was liable to do. Only problem was he had no speed. He'd flushed his stash before the cops showed up earlier that morning. And now his head felt like it was in a vise. The walls felt like they were closing in on him, and J.W.'s phone ringing off the hook wasn't helping matters. Jerry Lee tried watching television but quickly lost interest. The phone rang some more. GOD DAMN that phone! The fire in his belly began to roil. Jerry Lee grabbed the phone. Picked up the receiver, held down the switch, waited until he got a dial tone and rang up Hernando's Hide Away. When the bartender answered, Jerry Lee was short and to the point.

"Hey-uh, izza Killer. You holding? Uh-huh. Got any rigs? God-damn cops cleaned me out!"

Satisfied with the answer on the other end of the line, Jerry Lee sat on J.W.'s couch, secure in the notion that he would be high in no time. There was a moment of calm. Until the phone rang again. Almost immediately. Jerry Lee snatched it up without thinking and pitched it against the wall, mercifully ending its incessant wail.

There was no coming back from it for Shawn. Jerry Lee no longer needed to worry about high school sweethearts busting up his hillbilly hamlet or messing with the emotional cocktail he'd been nursing since his days as a child back in Ferriday, sitting in fear of the Lord, in fear of what he felt brewing inside him. It was a cock-tail Jerry Lee would nurse his whole life; an emotional speedball, really. It traded on equal parts self-confidence, God-given talent, fear of your maker, and the shame of being a mere mortal. With Shawn's death, shame and jealousy were on the run, and pride was once again creeping up the back stretch.

In the days after Shawn's death, Jerry Lee kept himself jacked on Talwin and thus speeding ahead of the hellfire spreading inside of him. The funeral was tough. Jerry Lee barely made it through. Being around Shawn's parents was too much. He said little, but somehow everything was still about him at the funeral. The prayers, the hymns, and even the people who got up to speak, they just spoke about Jerry Lee and the challenges he faced. Shawn's mother was outraged. Wasn't anybody going to eulogize her daughter?

That night, with the darkness closing in, Jerry Lee decided to call Shawn's sister, Denise. She picked up. Surprised to hear from her dead sister's husband, whose speech was slurred. He was clearly on one.

"Jesus Christ, Jerry Lee, what happened?"

"Denise…sissers daid an she uz a bad girl."

"What? What do you mean, Jerry? What do you mean?"

"Sheuzza badgirl…an she daid…"

Jerry Lee hung up. Passed out and woke up to another day in DeSoto County with seemingly endless possibilities. He wasted no time. That night, Jerry Lee was right back at it. Running from that hellfire. He was at Hernando's, his favorite bucket of blood, where there was always a seat open at the piano for him and where the spotlight always made him look ten feet tall and without a doubt more attractive than Elvis. It was at Hernando's piano where Jerry Lee made up a dirty little ditty on the spot and sang it with two beautiful women on the stool at his side: "I told her when she left me / I'd have another in her bed…"

The girls seemed to like it. Why wouldn't they? He was Jerry Lee Fucking Lewis! The Killer!!! He finished the song, got up off the piano bench, nodded to the band, and wobbled offstage down to his booth.

He was free. Free from guilt and free from suspicion. Despite the fact that one of the attending EMTs from the day Shawn's body was recovered filed a report stating that Jerry Lee had said, "We need to find out who killed——how she died." But Jerry Lee wasn't too interested in finding out how Shawn died or who might have killed her. The case was closed. The grand jury had decided no crime had occurred. Dr. Francisco, the private medical examiner okayed by Sheriff Sowell and paid for by Jerry Lee, determined there was no foul play. Finding drugs in her body after the autopsy's drug scans, he further determined that Shawn died from fluid in the lungs, a result of too much methadone. Eventually, the *Detroit Free Press* found itself up against too many sets of tight lips in DeSoto County and stopped pursuing Shawn's death as a crime—and the whole incident just went away.

The band picked up with a familiar Bo Diddley beat. "Who Do You Love?" The drummer put his backbone into it. Oh yeah! Jerry tapped his foot, but out of time with the beat. He was wasted. He thought to himself how he always loved Bo.

Bo beat Jerry Lee and Elvis to the devil's workshop by a couple of years. Yeah, Bo was one of the originals. Like Jerry Lee, he was a bad, bad man. Jerry Lee laughed to himself thinking of Bo's appearance on *The Ed Sullivan Show*. Bo slayed. But backstage, Sullivan, epic prick that he was, raged at Bo for playing his signature "Bo Diddley" song instead of his version of "Sixteen Tons," which they'd apparently agreed upon in preproduction. Sullivan was pissed. Bo, in interviews over the years, never hid his disdain for Sullivan but he always couched the truth. Bo always said Ed called him a double-crossing "black boy," but word around the early rock 'n' roll circuit back in the day was that what Ed called Bo was something far worse and that Bo had to be restrained from tearing Sullivan apart. Ed Sullivan! Sheeeeit. Bo never appeared on his show again. He was his own man. Did his own thing and rocked harder than most. Jerry Lee could appreciate that. Shit, maybe Bo had that hellfire? Maybe Bo was touched, too? The band played on:

> *I rode a lion to town, use a rattlesnake whip*
> *Take it easy, Arlene don't you give me no lip.*
> *Who do you love? Who do you love?*

Good question. Jerry Lee had no idea. He set his head on his forearm on top of Hernando's beer-soaked table and passed out.

CHAPTER 3

DEAD, EURONYMOUS, AND VARG

PER OHLIN WAS RIVETED. He was eighteen years old, sitting on his mom's sofa, staring at the television. This movie had been on before. The movie about the big black man from America who had that weird box of a guitar and played that old-style music his dad liked. Being a local product, the movie, a Swedish documentary, entitled *Bo Diddley, the Locomotor: I Don't Sound Like Nobody*, was constantly repeated on Swedish TV. Per couldn't have avoided it if he tried. And he did. Try to avoid it, that is. Because the music and the man making it couldn't have been less interesting to him. But today, when he'd awoken on his living room couch from his after-school nap, the television had been on and of course, the Bo Diddley movie was playing, and this time something different caught Per's eye. It was an interview with the artist, subtitled in Swedish, but Bo's laid-back Chicago drawl was slow enough for Per to understand anyway. And despite the language barrier and the fact that Per had difficulty relating to anybody at all, he began to feel like he could deeply understand the foreign man talking to him through the television.

Off the stage and freed from the stale, out-of-date, unexciting traditional music tropes that his rabid Swedish audience relied upon him to deliver, Bo Diddley was actually an interesting guy. He was big. Big head. Big black hat. Big glasses. Big shoulders and big hands. And his speaking voice was infinitely more interesting to Per than his singing voice. His speaking voice had a casual menace to it as he recounted where he'd found inspiration for his most famous song, a song Per had heard a million times but never thought twice of, "Who Do You Love?"

Given context, the song suddenly had meaning for Per: The young eccentric, delicate blond Swedish boy who'd been bullied mercilessly at school. Diddley was explaining what the kids in his neighborhood back in Chicago called, "signifying." A game of verbal insults where one kid would call another a name and then the other would respond upping the ante with an even harsher insult until either hilarity or a beating ensued. Per could identify with this. As of late, he'd been called unthinkable names at school: *skitstövel* (translated literally as "a boot full of shit" or "poop boot") and *bög* (Swedish for "fag"), or *dra åt skogen*, which translates to "Go to the forest," but should be taken more as "Go to hell," and for Per, this would prove to be a welcome destination.

Bo went on to explain that one day, while he himself was just a teenager and in search of music to express himself—music to ride out of his ghetto reality on—he sat, guitar in his lap, up in his apartment on the South Side of Chicago waiting on a song. His windows were open, and he heard some younger kids outside signifying—in Bo's words, "talking about each other like dogs." Yo Mama jokes. Sister jokes. Grandma jokes. Nothing was off-limits. At first, Bo thought it funny but as he listened more closely, he noticed there was a pattern to the way the kids spoke out these insults: back and forth to each other. They were sing-songing them. A rhythm had developed. And a melody:

Dah dum, dat, dat dah da dat dah da da
Dah da da da-dada da da dat dah
Do do do do…who do you love…

And the words…the insults…

Kid no. 1:   "Yo mama's got a tombstone hand and a graveyard mind."
Kid no. 2:   "Yeah, well, yo mama's just twenty-two and her pussy's all mine."

THAT WAS IT! Bo had it. His song. Of course the lyrics would need to be cleaned up a bit, but it was all there. Right outside his window. And now, for young Per Ohlin the once stale traditional, old-fashioned rock 'n' roll song had meaning:

I walk forty-seven miles of barbed wire,
I use a cobra snake for a necktie,
I got a brand-new house on the roadside,
Made from rattlesnake hide.
I got a brand-new chimney made on top,
Made out of a human skull.
Now come on take a walk with me, Arlene,
And tell me, who do you love?

Jesus Christ, Per thought. This shit sounded mean. By now, well into his adolescence and beginning his teenage rebellion, Per began channeling his own meanness into music. It was an instinctual reaction to the bullying. And it was cathartic. As the frontman for the Swedish band Morbid, he was honing his stagecraft, fucked-up as it was. He was hell-bent on making his own mark by stapling obituaries from the newspaper to his T-shirt, outfitting the stage with candles and borrowed coffins and doing whatever he could to shock his would-be audience and prove to the world that he belonged and that he was evil as fuck. So here, now, in front of his television, this Bo Diddley hoodoo shit really got him.

Bo Diddley's "Who Do You Love?" was released in 1956 in America, into a country reeling from the shock waves of rock 'n' roll. Parents, teachers, and squares everywhere warned of the new music's influence on the clean-cut youth of Eisenhower's postwar, conformist America. Surely this rebellious-sounding noise would cause kids to grow their hair, smoke reefer, have sex in public, worship Satan, and die. The squares were right. That was exactly what happened.

A decade later, kids were uniformly long-haired, smoking copious amounts of dope, and taking the pill. By 1969 they were sympathizing with the devil at Altamont, by the '70s they were burning their bras in Times Square. And by the '80s, cocaine, crack, and AIDS would claim countless young lives. Finally, by the '90s— 1991, to be exact—a heavy metal musician from Norway would go Bo Diddley one better, but it wouldn't be a chimney he'd make out of a human skull: It would be a necklace, made out of the skull of a Swedish boy with a morbid curiosity and one-time obsession with Bo Diddley.

Now come on take a walk with me, Arlene
And tell me, who do you love?

Bo Diddley's lyric may sound tame now, but it took a mere thirty-five years before its influence was brought to life in horrific fashion. Rebellion is metastatic. One generation's rebellion is another generation's norm. The line in the sand of what is and isn't acceptable gets redrawn with each new generation.

Bo Diddley was a descendent of bluesman Robert Johnson, who, hack rock journalists will eagerly tell you, sold his soul to the devil.

And Diddley's voodoo-esque braggadocio went on to inspire count-less classic rockers, including Satanic sympathizers Led Zeppelin, whose unabashed admiration for known Satanist Aleister Crowley and melding of steroidal Delta blues and Viking rock made it rain royalty checks. In 1974, even Elvis Presley, the King of Rock 'n' Roll, had to acknowledge, "Well, I may not be Led Zeppelin but I can still pack 'em in." Later that year, the King would find himself face-to-face with the mighty Led Zeppelin in his hotel suite. Zeppelin had attended one of his schmaltzy late-career Vegas shows, and the boys in the band were eager to meet their hero. When they did, *Elvis* asked *them* for *their* autographs! It was supposedly for his daughter, but still, the boys were freaked out. Where had they arrived? Where had we all arrived as a culture with Elvis Presley bowing to Led Zeppelin?

But the mutual lovefest wouldn't last. Within no time, a chill overtook Elvis's hotel suite when his manager, Colonel Tom Parker, entered. He surveyed the room and got wind of what was going on; his star attraction was prostrating himself to a bunch of longhairs. What in God's hell? The Colonel shook his head, rolled his eyes, and ushered the longhairs out the door before the King humbled himself any further to his heirs apparent.

Led Zeppelin's ascent was inspiring to not only Elvis and his daughter but to countless young bands. Their flirtation with Crowley and the dark arts in particular inspired another band from England, named Venom, to take it all one step further: to full-on devil *worship*. With song titles like, "In League with Satan," "Leave Me in Hell," and "1,000 Days in Sodom," Venom went on to influence an entirely new generation of metal bands like Metallica, Slayer, and Testament until finally inspiring a completely new subgenre of heavy metal called black metal.

Black metal was started by Norwegian teenagers unable to stand the strains of conformity, boredom, anonymity, and long, dark winters. Norway, a small constitutional monarchy, went through a brief Viking phase during its adolescence, flirted with fascism in its young adulthood, and eventually settled lazily into a type of democratic socialism during middle age. Though small, it's one of the world's richest countries. The state takes care of its own: Government bureaucracy employs 30 percent of the country. Disability pensions for the unemployed are easy to come by. There's not a lot of poverty. There's not a lot of income disparity. The crime rate is low, and punishments for the crimes that people do commit are lenient. The country's greatest cultural export is frozen fish. Historically, there's not a lot to get pissed off about, because there's not a lot that goes on in Norway. Norway is kind of like Europe's answer to an American flyover state. In short, if you're a Norwegian teenager you're probably bored. And even worse than that, you're probably bored without a whole lot to rebel against.

If there's one indisputable truth in the Holy Bible, you'll probably find it in Proverbs 16:27: "Idle hands are the devil's workshop."

Without overt societal injustice, Norwegian teenagers looked to their heritage for something to rebel against. Inspired by Venom, Bathory, and a growing group of Satanic-influenced heavy metal bands in the 1980s, Norwegian teenagers saw their country's Christian heritage as a reason to rebel.

In a moralistic Christian society, worshiping Satan is just about the strongest form of rebellion one can take. Mix in nihilism, Nazism, ancient Norse Viking mythology, paganism, blistering blast beats, and speaker-shredding power chords, and you've got a powerful elixir of teenage angst.

Black metal became a tangible and legitimate force on August 16, 1987, with the release of the *Deathcrush* demo by the Norwegian band Mayhem. Critics may point to Mayhem's officially released first full-length album, *De Mysteriis Dom Sathanas*, as black metal's genre-defining record, but it has none of the charm of the earlier *Deathcrush* demo. *Deathcrush* sounds less like a band trying to make something and more like a bunch of extremely pent-up kids bashing shit around in their basement in front of crappy microphones that just happen to be pointed toward their half-broken amplifiers. Mayhem's demo—with its lo-fi, high-energy metal recording—doesn't sound like anything that came before it. It sounds bleak, and primitive. It sounds, in a word, *cold*. *Deathcrush* is inspired and inspiring. It was the landmark black metal recording that would compel hordes of bands to come.

Per Ohlin was doing his best to warm his feet over Satan's burning embers back in Sweden. But he was frustrated. His Morbid bandmates weren't as committed to a lifestyle that was "morbid" in every fashion. So, upon hearing the *Deathcrush* demo, Per developed a sort of crush himself. A band crush, but a crush nonetheless. These guys got it, he thought.

Bleed down to the fucking core
You're going down for fucking more.

This is what Per was talking about. He vibed on the lyrics to "Chainsaw Gutfuck," from Mayhem's *Deathcrush*, and thought of the tall boys at school with the broad shoulders, short hair, and impeccable complexions who tortured him with daily insults for, well, just being him; long-haired and into music. Fuck them, Per thought. He longed to see them bleed out. And he was sure the dudes in Mayhem would agree with him.

As obsessed underground music fans did in the days before the internet, Per began to correspond with his new favorite band, Mayhem, by mail. Per was eager to make a connection and to show them that he wasn't just some ordinary fanboy, so he mailed them a cassette of him singing with Morbid. This way they'd know he had talent. And to prove that he wasn't fucking around, that he was truly evil like they were, Per included, along with the cassette, a mouse he crucified. The members of Mayhem were sufficiently impressed. So at the age of nineteen, Per moved from Sweden to Norway to sing in Mayhem. He wasn't the band's original singer, but he would prove to be its most legendary.

The bullying that Per Ohlin experienced as a child produced in him a darkness. He fed that darkness by obsessing over death. Ohlin was so obsessed with death that he changed his name, unequivocally, to "Dead." He claimed he'd wanted to die ever since he was three years old. Once he became a full member of Mayhem, Dead committed to the role in a way that would make most method actors feel inadequate. To prepare for Mayhem gigs, Dead would bury his clothes in the ground so that when he eventually wore them onstage, they'd have the stench of the earth on them, just as a corpse would. Before shows he'd walk around inhaling the rotting carcass of a crow he carried with him in a bag because he wanted the smell of death in his nostrils when he performed. And during Mayhem gigs, he'd ghoulishly display pigs' heads on stakes at the foot of the stage.

While performing, Dead would cut himself, dousing bandmates, himself, and the remaining audience members with his blood. He wore all black, and like most metalheads, he had a taste for denim, leather, studs, and spikes. He painted his face white and blackened the area around his eyes to look more like a corpse. Not in a theatrical Alice Cooper or KISS way, but in a "scary as All Hallows' Eve" way.

With Dead fronting Mayhem, the band's reputation and influence expanded, and Norway's black metal scene grew wings. Its pilot was Dead's bandmate and Mayhem's founding guitarist, Øystein Aarseth. Aarseth was the charismatic leader of the Norwegian black metal scene. Before founding Mayhem and Deathlike Silence Productions, the record label that released Mayhem's records, Aarseth changed his name to "Euronymous" to complete his transformation from polite upper-middle-class Norwegian boy into full-blown black metal king.

And heavy lay the crown. Euronymous proudly presented himself as king of the black metal scene, stating that he "was black metal" and that "black metal is me." But underneath the carefully cultivated image of an antisocial communist who hated humanity lay something quite different. Despite the fact that he identified as evil, anti-humanist, and someone against any and all forms of human pleasure, Euronymous was a mere mortal and needed pleasures of the flesh just like anybody else. His preference was for men, but in the black metal community that sort of expression would have been cause for expulsion. The result of suppressing his desires: an overcompensation of sorts. He made and sold some of the meanest, heaviest, most testosterone-fueled music in the world. Gay was not evil, and he, Euronymous was the most evil. The most black metal.

Euronymous and Dead were joined at the hip. Both bearing a lifetime of inner turmoil of different varieties, they bonded easily. They were not only bandmates, but also roommates. They listened to Motörhead and Bathory records, talked politics, and dissed poser commercial metal bands like Death Angel and Napalm Death as they plotted a path for their band and their scene to rise to infamy. The hopes-and-dreams portion of their story didn't last.

As Mayhem's career didn't take off the way Dead hoped it would, the two argued frequently, bickering like an old married couple. And when Euronymous annoyed him, Dead would sleep in the forest outside their cabin (*dra åt skogen*, or "Go to the forest"). Dead became more and more withdrawn. He was likely clinically depressed, but this was a time, a place, and a scene where such self-awareness was not allowed.

Given Dead's state of mind, his behavior, and his fascination with death, it's possible that he suffered from what is known as Cotard delusion, a rare mental illness in which the affected person believes that they are dead; that they are actually a walking, putrefying corpse. This illness manifests after a life-threatening trauma like the beatings Dead took as a schoolboy—in particular, the one where he ended up in the hospital with a ruptured spleen; an experience that left him clinically dead for a period of time. Whatever the reason, his obsession with death became all-consuming. He got his hands on some snuff films on VHS. He watched them. Then he watched them again…and again. He sat alone in his room and cut himself. He stopped eating in an effort to obtain starving wounds. He told friends he believed that his blood had frozen in his veins, that he was a nonhuman and didn't belong on Earth. That he'd died as a child and longed for the deep sleep he'd experienced for a brief period then.

Cotard delusion or not, deep down Dead was dealing with demons. An intense hatred for authority, social constructs, and ultimately himself were all manifested from his experiences as a misunderstood and, ultimately, bullied child. Playing in Mayhem provided a vent, but the demons within Dead would eventually prove to be too much.

On April 8, 1991, Per Ohlin, aka Dead, singer of Mayhem, the world's preeminent black metal band, sat down on his sofa and began to write a note. It started with "Excuse all the blood…"

When authorities found the note, Dead's blood was indeed in need of an excuse. It was everywhere. Dead had slit his wrists. Then, he slit his own throat. And somehow, after all of that, he managed to fire off a shot from a shotgun directly into his forehead.

Dead was dead, at twenty-two years old.

I've got a tombstone hand and a graveyard mind.
I'm just twenty-two and I don't mind dying.

Dead also noted in his farewell that "it was the intention that I would die in the woods so that it would take a few days before I was possibly found. I belong in the woods and have always done so." But Euronymous was glad that his friend decided to end it all in a place where it didn't take "a few days" to find him. His bandmate discovered Dead's body. He assessed the situation with the cold dispassion of a grizzled homicide detective, and then he acted quickly.

Not to call authorities or family. Instead he moved out the door and down the street to purchase a disposable camera. He high-tailed it back to the apartment, where Dead's exploded skull and bloodied body lay in the early stages of rigor mortis, and began taking pictures. Euronymous knew a good album cover when he saw one. He then collected bits of his friend's skull and brain. The shards from the skull would make for great necklaces, he thought. Euronymous would later boil the bits of brain down into a stew and consume them so that he could claim the vaunted status of a cannibal.

From beyond this mortal coil, Dead likely sensed that his friend Euronymous had cannibalized what was left of his brain matter. There was no anger in the afterlife. No disgust. In fact, quite the opposite. Dead was impressed with his former bandmate's commitment to evil. Dead even found it funny that, in life, Euronymous had never been given the chance to consummate his love for Dead—but now in death, he was literally consuming him. If Euronymous was indeed gay, Dead thought, he was one evil motherfucker. Let's see those *rævhåls* in Napalm Death eat some brains.

Dead's grisly suicide would be immortalized on the cover of Mayhem's 1995 live bootleg, *Dawn of the Black Hearts*. The photo is arresting. It's the type of thing you wish you could unsee but you can't. The irony, of course, is that it is a "live" album with a real-life picture of a dead guy named Dead on the cover. The album's closing track is one of Mayhem's first compositions, "Pure Fucking Armageddon"—and pure fucking armageddon was exactly what the black metal scene was about to unleash onto Norway.

The way the architects of the black metal scene saw it, to be from Norway in the early '90s and to be truly into black metal meant that you had to be *truly evil*. The type of evil that went way beyond the B-grade horror-movie lyrics from Black Sabbath. The type of evil that was much scarier than some long-haired skateboarders in baggy shorts and painter's caps listening to Anthrax and crushing cans of Meister Bräu on a school night. To be truly "black metal" meant you had to live for death. You praised Satan. You declared war on society and all things moral, particularly Christianity. You listened to and made raw, primitive-sounding, noncommercial heavy metal. The goal for Norwegian black metalheads was to completely subvert democratic morality; to banish poser metal bands who didn't take death and destruction

Euronymous consuming the brains of his dead bandmate, Per Ohlin.

seriously back to the punk rock ghettos they crawled out of. So forget about Napalm Death and fuck Anthrax.

With Dead's death there formed a vacuum of charisma in the scene Euronymous lorded over. Soon a new fresh-faced personality came along: Varg Vikernes, aka "Count Grishnackh," the one-man engine behind the new and exciting black metal band, Burzum. Euronymous was taken with the intensely handsome and talented Count, and he agreed to release Burzum's records on Deathlike Silence Productions. Varg—through the strength of his Manson-esque gaze and the excitement of his new band—quickly ascended to an unofficial leadership role in the fast-growing scene that now included a flock of new bands like Darkthrone, Immortal, and Enslaved.

Varg's Burzum lyrics give insight into what made Count Grish-nackh tick.

This is WAR!...
Many wounded crawl helplessly around
On the bloodred snowy ground.
WAR!

Varg Vikernes took his music and himself seriously. He wasn't in this for the free beer or to bust skateboarders with Death Angel patches in the grill with fisted rolls of coins in a street fight. No, Varg was in this for the War. He'd been raging against the hypocrites ever since his days as a boy in Baghdad, when his dad, a computer programmer, worked for Saddam Hussein. Varg had zero respect for the Iraqis. He was disgusted by how easily they subverted their own interests to his white family. Even at the young age of twelve, it was obvious to Varg that the white man had the power. Varg refused to hide the fact. Unlike his father, who was as racist as the day was long—he collected WWII Nazi memorabilia and held among his prized possessions an authentic Nazi flag—yet would have none of it when Varg became involved with the Nazi skinhead movement after they returned from Iraq.

Dead, from beyond the grave, knew Varg and Euronymous would click. Varg was like a better-looking version of Dead, but his hatred was pointed outward, where Dead's aimed straight back at himself. Varg quickly committed himself with a fury to the black metal scene. He rose to the occasion to play bass for Mayhem, after Jørn "Necrobutcher" Stubberud quit, understandably freaked out by Dead's suicide and its gratuitously gory aftermath. But Varg's commitment to the cause inextricably infused black metal's Satanism with his even more toxic and racist ethno-nationalism. In addition to his experiences as a boy in Iraq, Varg believed Christianity had purged Norway of its heritage by casting aside Norse tradition, so he took this shit personally. Varg Vikernes was out for revenge against Christians, blacks, homosexuals, posers, and basically anyone who wasn't a nihilistic, blue-eyed, pagan metalhead. His dad was a hypocrite. It was the last thing Varg wanted to be. He'd play the part to its fullest. Dead may have been dead, but even he was impressed by Varg's commitment.

Varg sat with Euronymous behind the counter of his record shop, Helvete—which in Norwegian translates to "Hell." Helvete served as a meeting place for all of the black metal scensters. Euronymous, in addition to using Helvete as headquarters for his record label, would also use the venue to flex his big man on the black metal campus credentials. Some of these younger black metalheads (especially the handsome ones) needed to know who was in charge, so Euronymous would puff his chest out in front of them and pick winners and losers; which new bands to sign, when to release the next Burzum album, where Mayhem should play live, and occasionally pop off some there-is-nothing-more-evil-than-black-metal manifesto. But with Dead dead and Varg on the scene, the ideological rhetoric was largely Varg's side of the street, so Euronymous's manifesto was more of a casual social chorus that went something like this: "Fuck Metallica. Fuck everyone, actually—Metallica, Slayer, the blacks, the Jews, everyone. Long live Satan. Black metal rules." That sort of thing. The group assembled at Helvete would later come to be called "the Black Circle." On this day, Euronymous, Varg, and the rest of the crew were closing up shop early to head to Oslo to check out a Morbid Angel show.

Between the opening and headlining acts, Euronymous, Varg, and others from the Black Circle hung outside the club smoking cigarettes and lamenting how lame the scene had become. How there were no bands who were truly evil. Corpse paint, pigs' heads onstage, and Satanic lyrics churned through guttural screaming vocals weren't enough to inspire other bands beyond Norway's black metal scene to carry the torch for evil. Something else had to be done. The ante needed to be upped. Varg had done little beyond talk racist shit to prove his evil bona fides, and ever since Dead's death, the Norwegian black metal scene had begun to look ordinary. Like just a bunch of teenagers fucking around with distortion pedals and their mother's makeup kits. If the scene was going to grow, then something dramatic needed to happen to inspire more metalheads to turn to evil.

After his death, Dead knew that Euronymous had grown soft. His cannibalism aside, Euronymous was more interested in keeping up appearances than in truly leading the black metal scene into the future. Dead knew that Varg was the scene's only hope. If black metal was going to survive and grow beyond the poser confines of other heavy metal subgenres, then real leadership was needed. But Varg needed a push, so Dead whispered to Varg a wicked idea. It was pure evil. And if implemented correctly, it would bring Norway to its knees and show the world what the black metal scene was really all about: Pure Fucking Armageddon.

Shortly after that fateful night outside the Morbid Angel show, in the peaceful villages of Bekkestien and Kråkstad, townsfolk began to find graves of their relatives vandalized. In addition, the home of Christofer Johnsson, the front man for so-called "death metal" band Therion had been set on fire. A note was stuck to his door with a knife. It read, "The Count was here and he will come back." A homosexual man in Lillehammer was killed randomly, stabbed more than thirty times and left to bleed out in the woods. Dead knew the death of the homosexual would rattle Euronymous to his core no matter how deeply ensconced he may have been in his closet. Then the church fires started.

The first church to go up in flames was the Fantoft Stave Church, one of Norway's historic treasures. It made national headlines. Next? The Revheim Church. Then the Holmenkollen Chapel and the Ormoya Church.

Satanic symbols started showing up around the sites of the burnings.

Norwegians had no idea what was happening. The press covered the arsons breathlessly. And as the coverage expanded, more churches burned. The black metal rebellion was on. Norwegian black metalheads were literally carrying a torch for their scene, and black metal was no longer a B-grade horror flick: It was full-on evil. Real evil.

Scenesters became heads of arson squads continuously trying to outdo one another. More churches burned: The Skjold Church. The Hauketo Church. The Old Åsane Church. The Methodist church in Sarpsborg; that one took the life of a firefighter. More than thirty churches had been set ablaze. Due to the desecrated graves and Satanic vandalism discovered at the burn scenes, the press blamed it on an until now unknown, unnamed, unimaginable clan of Satanists.

But authorities were slow to pounce on the Satanist theory. Some held out hope that all the fires—and the other assorted crimes—were all just a big accidental coincidence. The bottom line? Nobody had a clue who was behind the terror. Fear was rampant, and there was no real boogeyman in sight.

Not until January 1993 anyway. That's when Varg Vikernes decided he had enough with the false rumors surrounding the church burnings. The rumor was that Euronymous had masterminded them. Varg seethed with rage. He couldn't let Euronymous take the credit for what he had pulled off (with a little influence from a certain dark spirit).

Varg decided to try to cheekily set the record straight by giving an interview to a daily newspaper. In it, he claimed he knew who burned the churches *and* who murdered the homosexual man in Lillehammer. It took local police about five minutes to identify Varg—with his penchant for being photographed with torches, knives, chain mail, and long hair—as a person of interest, and it wasn't long before they were on to the entire scene.

Within no time, authorities had found a flyer promoting Burzum's new album, aptly titled *Ashes*. On it, there was an image depicting the burning of Fantoft Stave Church. The flyer also, unbelievably, included Varg's address. Dead laughed from beyond the grave because, you know, there were so many people coming upon black metal flyers and deciding they absolutely *needed* to send their hard-earned cash to get a copy of the latest album by a band they probably never heard of. Dead thought that for all Varg's supposed high-minded Norse Viking neoracist, pseudo-intellectual horseshit, the Count sure seemed like a fucking moron when it came right down to it. The police showed up at the address on the flyer and found Varg holed up with enough explosives to blast them all to hell. He was taken into custody before he could use the explosives to blow up the Nidaros Cathedral, as he was planning, in celebration of Mayhem's next album. Now *that's* how you throw a record release party!

Remarkably, Varg was released for lack of evidence, but not before the rumors took off and the kids in the scene got wind of who the real mastermind was. Euronymous roiled with jealousy while Varg's ego soared. Varg's long-simmering distrust of Euronymous was now brimming over into barely containable contempt. The originator of the black metal scene no longer seemed that evil. Not to Varg or anybody within the Black Circle. The vain grab for credit for the church burnings was a big wake-up call for the scene. And soon another set of rumors took flight that would further discredit Euronymous. There were rumors that he was gay, and that someone had even found VHS tapes of gay porn that belonged to him. Rumors that he was secretly in love with Dead and that he pressured Dead to kill himself because he couldn't stand it anymore. There was another rumor that Euronymous actually pulled the trigger and killed Dead. That he and Dead were in a quarrel over something of Euronymous's that Dead had found; VHS tapes with gay porn and a dildo.

Varg considered the rumors against his own friendship with Euronymous. After all, Euronymous had welcomed Varg into the scene in the first place, but if he would stoop so low as to pretend to be the one behind the church burnings, what else was he faking? As

Varg, Euronymous and Dead: Three-headed black metal monster.

Varg thought about it, he realized a lot of Euronymous's identity seemed fabricated. While Varg was a devoted follower of Stalin and Hitler's SS, Euronymous was a socialist who collected government welfare and still took money from his parents.

And if all of that wasn't enough, Euronymous owed Varg money for unpaid Burzum royalties.

Then Varg heard a final rumor, this one more far-fetched than the last batch, that Euronymous was planning on kidnapping Varg, torturing him, filming the torture, and then finally killing him on film. Even though Euronymous seemed like a poser to Varg, Varg could imagine his former friend in such a desperate state that he would do anything to convince the world that he was every bit as evil as they once thought he was. Euronymous's reputation was shit, and reputation was all he cared about. Plus, killing Varg would take care of that debt.

Dead, still dead, delighted in the conflict. He sensed Varg brimming with rage and Euronymous overflowing with jealousy of Varg's new status in the scene. A scene that Euronymous believed he alone built and defined, and that defined him.

Meanwhile, the circumstances around Dead's suicide, the rumors of Euronymous's cannibalism, the church burnings, the grave dese-crations, the rumored death of a homosexual man at the hands of someone in the scene, and the harassment of other poser metal bands all caused Mayhem's reputation to ring out worldwide.

But a snuff film? Showing the torture and murder of one of the scene's biggest stars? That would really be something: true evil. Let's see Dave Mustaine rub out James Hetfield on film. Megadeth? More like megapussies.

Varg was enraged. First of all, because he hadn't been the one to think of it. Secondly, he wasn't going to let a brown-eyed, socialist, closet homosexual who owed him money get over on him. Euronymous needed to be confronted.

August 10, 1993. Varg Vikernes turned up at Euronymous's apartment unannounced at three in the morning, under the guise of signing his next Burzum record contract. This was something that Euronymous, despite the time of night, was very keen on making happen. Burzum was one of his record label's main moneymakers. Without a signed contract, there were no royalties to collect.

He buzzed Varg in to let him up to his fourth-floor apartment. It would prove to be a crucial mistake.

Varg wasn't there to sign any papers. He was there to put an end to this beef, one way or another. Secure in the fact that his hunting knife was nestled snugly in his pocket.

Euronymous opened the door in his underwear. Varg would later testify that when he asked Euronymous about his plans to murder him, Euronymous responded by kicking him in the chest.

Varg was stunned. He grabbed Euronymous and threw him to the floor. Euronymous quickly got to his feet and ran toward the kitchen.

Varg assumed it was to grab a knife or some other sort of weapon. Maybe the shotgun that Dead shot himself with: Varg knew Euronymous kept it handy.

The Count was not afraid: he was determined. Determined to not be murdered by this poser. Determined, instead, to take *his* life. To survive. It was his nature. He grabbed his own knife and took off after Euronymous, catching up to him before he could find a weapon. Varg stabbed him. But Euronymous managed to keep moving, back toward the door and out of the apartment. He broke down the hallway, screaming for help and ringing as many doorbells as he could along the way.

Varg was hot on his trail. Close enough to continue stabbing him all the way down the stairwell. Euronymous could do little, but he somehow stayed on his feet.

His momentum kept hurtling him down the stairs.

His adrenaline kept the screams for help coming at a piercing volume.

The horrific sounds kept the neighbors terrified and paralyzed in their apartments.

Varg's hate kept the stabbings coming: twenty-two of them, until Euronymous could run no more.

His momentum slowed. He staggered to a wobbling standstill for a second or two before falling to his knees. Bloodied and gasping for breath, he looked up to face his murderer: his one-time friend and comrade-in-arms, Count Grishnackh, who then took his knife in both of his hands, raised it above his head and silently called upon the great Norse god of thunder. Then, with the pure Viking rage that was his lineage, Varg brought the knife down straight into Euronymous's skull.

He died instantly.

Varg was arrested nine days later. An informant gave authorities all they needed on Varg for the murder and the church burnings. Another member of the scene, Bard "Faust" Eithun, drummer from the black metal band Emperor, admitted to the murder of the homosexual man in Lillehammer's Olympic park. He claimed he just "wanted to see what killing a man felt like." He got eight years. For killing a man in cold blood. Dead mused about what was more wicked: the murder or the lack of justice.

Pure evil. With little consequence.

Varg pleaded innocent to all of the charges and turned his trial into a sideshow that no doubt made Charlie Manson proud; playing the role of Satanist, neofascist, and pagan warlord. Basically, if the rebellious shoe fit, Varg wore it. The press ate it all up, quickly making Count Grishnackh Norway's public enemy number one.

Varg Vikernes was convicted for arson for three of the more

than thirty church burnings, attempted arson of a fourth, possession of illegal explosives, and the murder of Euronymous. He was sentenced to twenty-one years in prison, which, unbelievably, is the maximum penalty allowed in Norway for murder and arson.

Pure evil. With little consequence.

Today Norwegian black metal is bigger than ever. Second-generation bands like Gorgoroth have taken the genre far beyond the cold, dark Norwegian forest, to every corner of the world.

The horrors carried out by Dead, Euronymous, Varg, and others from the original black metal scene built a notorious reputation for the genre to attract new generations of followers with.

Mayhem still sells records and still tours. Sure it's with the one original member and yeah, their shows these days have more in common with a Fat Elvis Vegas Revue than they do the *Dawn of the Black Hearts* bootleg, but despite—or possibly because of— the band's horrific acts, there is a large and active international audience for Norwegian black metal; a genre of music that was built on a foundation of murder, arson, cannibalism, and what can only be described as the most extreme form of musical rebellion to ever exist.

Dead thought about all of this from inside the back of Mayhem's fast-moving tour bus. Dead, of course, was dead. None of the current members of the band knew of his presence, but they could feel it on some deeper level. It was more like the cold sweat of realizing a forgotten shame than a haunted feeling. And Dead was surprised with how far the band and the black metal scene had come. He took in the passing cars out the window and let his mind wander. "Evil." His bandmates weren't evil. They weren't antisocial. Here in the present, at the end of the day they were entertainers. They were fucking capitalists. Out here crisscrossing the United States playing sold-out shows and selling boxes upon boxes of concert T-shirts with the now-iconic Mayhem logo in the trademarked black-metal font on them. Satanists? Nah. Opportunists. These days, Mayhem has more in common with Elvis Presley or Bo Diddley than Venom or Aleister Crowley.

The sudden roar of the pursuing choppers on the interstate behind their bus pushed these thoughts away. A gang of Hells Angels on Harley-Davidsons pulled up alongside the tour bus at seventy miles per hour, their bikes roaring like majestic beasts. The "Hells Angels." What a name. What a sight, he thought. Now *that's* evil.

CHAPTER 4

GRAM PARSONS

GRAM PARSONS HELD ON tight and wrapped his arms around the torso of a burly Hells Angel named Tiny. Tiny's chopper spit dust from the dry California earth indiscriminately. The bike roared. Sitting on the back of it, the back of his head resting on the sissy bar, and holding on for dear life, Gram Parsons's skull hurt. He felt the egg start to swell. He knew he should have worn a helmet. But Tiny didn't have an extra brain bucket. His old lady had split and took it with her. So Gram took his chances as he hopped on the back of Tiny's chopper out on Interstate 580 and spun off for Altamont Speedway, with his dome exposed and his shiny, shoulder-length caramel hair flowing in the northern California wind.

Gram looked good today. He knew it. And he had to. It was a big day. It wasn't every day that you and your band got to open for the Rolling Stones, the biggest, baddest rock 'n' roll band on the planet. But despite his confidence in his attire—embroidered halter top, snakeskin vest, silk bell bottoms that fit perfectly, and a tight puka shell necklace—Gram was rattled. His head *hurt*.

The sound of the chopper beneath him was loud, but hitching a ride on the back of a Hells Angel's chopper was a necessity.

Altamont was a shitshow. The Rolling Stones, at the time one of the world's biggest grossing concert attractions, wanted to give back to their fans, so a free concert was arranged. Hastily. In forty-eight hours. The concert was to be a sort of Woodstock for the West, albeit four months later and about twenty degrees colder. At least that was the idea being bandied about by Mick Jagger, whose hippie-dippie mumbo jumbo musing on the event couldn't have been more of the time. Leading up to Altamont, Jagger said, "It's creating a microcosmic society which sets examples for the rest of America as to how one can behave at large gatherings…The concert is an excuse for everyone to talk to each other, get together, sleep with each other, hold each other, and get very stoned." San Francisco's Golden Gate Park was the original idea but city authorities knew better, so in hurried fashion it was decided that Altamont Speedway—about sixty miles outside of San Francisco—would be the place.

One hundred thousand people were expected. Three hundred thousand showed up. Naturally there was a pileup on the freeway. There were simply too many people, too many cars for the road to hold, and so Interstate 580 became a parking lot. Gram Parsons and his bandmates, the Flying Burrito Brothers, were performing at Altamont in support of their excellent debut, *The Gilded Palace of Sin*, which was by definition a country album but had effortlessly crossed over to a mainstream rock 'n' roll audience. Gram and his band might have felt like they were on their way, but today, in the December dust of Northern California, they weren't going anywhere, having literally driven themselves off into a ditch. Gram was incensed. He wasn't going to miss this. He might have had a Byrd, Chris Hillman, in his band, but there was a bona fide Rolling Stone, his man-crush, Keith Richards, waiting for him backstage—if he could only get himself through the four-mile-long sea of people. So he flagged down the Hells Angel as soon as he saw him deftly maneuvering through the traffic and up along the side of the highway where Gram and the rest of his band had broken down.

Gram pleaded his case: He was a musician. He was with the Rolling Stones. He *needed* to get to the stage on time.

The Hells Angels were doing security—for the promise of $500 in beer—so they could come and go as they pleased, and their bikes made it possible for them to work their way through the mass of hippie humanity with little resistance. Tiny, the Hells Angel on the chopper, wanted to know how the rest of Gram's band was going to get to the stage on time. "Oh, they'll figure it out." Gram wasted no time, hopped on the back of the chopper, and Tiny quickly— too quickly—yanked the throttle. When he did, the bike shot forward with a short blast, and Gram's head shot back and violently banged into the bike's steel sissy bar behind him. For a second Gram saw stars. He blinked his eyes open and squinted through the dust being spit up by the walking concertgoers. He held his arms tight around Tiny's chest clad in his leather biker vest. The one with the red Hells Angels top rocker patch emblazoned across the back and the bottom rocker letters C-A-L-I-F-O-R-N-I-A bending below the immediately recognizable "Death's Head" logo and small, square "MC" patch.

Gram's head pounded. He focused on the song swirling around in his brain that morning: "Suspicious Minds" by Elvis Presley. The King was back. Thinking about it made Gram happy. The world was a better place with Elvis in it. Or at least with Elvis on top of the charts. Gram Parsons had a special affinity for Elvis Presley. He was a country boy like him. White, but steeped in blues and gospel music and burdened by the trappings of wealth—just like Gram was. Gram, of course, hadn't earned his money like Elvis had. Gram inherited it. He never knew the poverty Elvis came from: Gram's mom was Avis Snively, whose family was responsible for one-third of the citrus fruits exported out of Florida, so he was raised without ever having to worry about money. But he wasn't without worry completely. Gram *did* know the pain Elvis felt. Money solves a lot of problems, but deep-rooted emotional turmoil isn't one of them. He could always relate to the raw sadness that anchored the best of Elvis's songs and was comforted that in 1969, the Chips Moman–produced "Suspicious Minds" was sitting high upon the charts and the King was back.

We're caught in a trap
I can't walk out…

There were people everywhere. Something had to give if Gram was going to make it to the stage on time. Tiny moved his chopper from the highway up the hill to the entrance of the Speedway. Once atop the rise, a vista unfolded before them peppered with sun-stroked hippies setting up camp en masse. The Altamont Pass was in full display. Dusty. Hazed. Its grass burned by the sun and patrolled by rattlesnakes, it was beautiful in that "only in California" kind of way. Nestled next to the Diablo mountain range, on this day Altamont looked as good a place as any for the devil to set up shop.

Tiny accelerated down the hill. Gram held on tight. Tiny maneuvered the chopper around the stoned hippies frolicking and just beginning to feel the effects of the powerful, speed-laced Owsley Purple LSD that had begun circulating through the crowd early that day.

Gram was impressed with the way Tiny handled the powerful machine. Aside from the bumpy start—which was really more Gram's fault—the ride into the concert, though filled with fits and starts, was wildly efficient and wildly exhilarating.

Gram needed the excitement. His pain was real and, if he wasn't careful, all-consuming. It had been eleven years since his old man realized he couldn't see his way through and decided instead to bite down on the barrel of a shotgun, but the dreams haunted Gram. Back when the grief was new and especially raw, the dreams were vivid; literal nightmares depicting his father's suicide. But as time passed, his dreams took on a more fantastical nature. They were less violent but still entirely fucked-up. Death portals bent by the subconscious and forced open by unprocessed grief that horrified him.

As a boy, Gram sweated through his dreams until, while a student at Harvard, he discovered the benefit of LSD and the ability to *make* his own dreams.

He then found speed and the ability to outrun his nightmares.

And of course, there was always the old reliable benefit of booze and the ability it provided him to outdrink his nightmares.

And finally, if all of that failed, there was heroin and its ability to totally obliterate his nightmares altogether.

Self-medicating became a daily necessity, and today was no different. Gram needed to get backstage, find Keith, and get his head on straight before getting onstage.

Altamont Speedway was littered with stoned hippies lying on blankets, smoking grass, copping feels, blitzing out on acid, playing Frisbee, talking jive, talking revolution. Gram looked around in wonder. He sensed that Tiny couldn't give a fuck. Tiny was focused on the job at hand: getting Gram to the stage to see his friend the Rolling Stone before he himself went onstage. So Tiny punched it. He drove over blankets, through picnic baskets and foam coolers, all along the way kicking dust up into the faces of everyone they passed. And when some stoned college kid, ignorant to the job at hand, refused to get out of the way, Tiny would slow down and slowly scuff his front wheel up softly against the unsuspecting hippie's leg or foot while simultaneously giving a pull on the throttle and letting out a death growl from the chopper. It never failed. They'd get the message on the quick and get out of the way.

As they got closer to the stage the mass of people thickened. Tiny had to slow his chopper to a near stop. Gram moved his cowboy boots from the passenger pegs to the ground, slightly upsetting the balance of the bike. The stage area was in sight. Not the stage, though—it was only four feet tall!—but the stage *area*. A four-foot-tall stage. For three hundred thousand people. Hippie planning at its best.

The roar of the chopper parted the remaining audience members who were crammed at the foot of the stage. All that separated the audience from the band was a thin piece of twine. Gram's heart pulsed with excitement. Keith would be close. He could feel it. And he'd see Gram's new band and be blown away and then they'd go cop and party into the morning and after that, who knew what? Maybe Keith would produce Gram's next record? Maybe Keith would even ask Gram to join the Stones? Wild, Gram thought. Wild.

Finally, Tiny pulled his massive motorcycle up to a stop and parked it, literally, right in front of the stage. Gram hopped off without thanking Tiny for the Herculean task he'd just pulled off for him. Gram was too excited. Let's get into this, he thought. Where's Keith? He slipped under the twine and to the side of the stage. From the way he was dressed, it was obvious to the other Hells Angels running stage security that he belonged there. Tiny shook his head and cracked a beer. "Goddamn hippies."

Somehow, the rest of the Flying Burrito Brothers managed to find their way into the show and the backstage area. Gram searched for Keith but he was nowhere to be found, which meant neither was any heroin. Gram took some acid and pulled hard on a bottle of Jack Daniel's. Showtime arrived, and the Burrito Brothers jumped onstage under the California sunshine and dove into a speed-laced-LSD inspired version of the iconic truck-driving tune that Dave Dudley had made famous six years before, "Six Days on the Road." They sounded *great* and the crowd loved it. Those of them who could hear and see it, anyway.

After the set, Gram passed out backstage. When he came to, he was being rousted by Burrito Brothers guitar player Bernie Leadon, who was making the case in no uncertain terms that if they didn't get out of there now, with the Stones, in their helicopter, then they'd never get out and who knew what the hell would happen. The Hells Angels were on a rampage. Janked on cheap beer, speed, and acid, they'd taken to beating audience members with pool cues. Some kid pulled a gun and got stuck by an Angel and had bled out all over the festival grounds. Bad vibes. All around. You gotta move.

Gram shook it off, stood up, and got swept up in the movement and energy of the exiting entourage. People all around him were yelling. Screaming. Road crew. Angels. Fans. Entourage members. The mood was beyond dark. The look on the face of Stones drummer, Charlie Watts, said it all. Shit was bad. There was a dead kid in the middle of the Speedway's dance floor. Woodstock of the West, my ass. Altamont was more like a Hades holiday. The '60s were over, man, and tonight sealed it. Peace and love died on the dance floor tonight next to an eighteen-year-old named Meredith Hunter.

Before Gram knew it, he was jammed into the Stones helicopter next to the beautiful Mamas and Papas singer, Michelle Phillips. She roused something in Gram quick, the same thing she roused in most men—lust. Gram couldn't control himself, and without warning or conceit, and perhaps trying to spin the wheel one last time on the free-love decade, Gram took his chances and tried jamming his tongue down Michelle's throat. Remarkably, she played it cool. She squirmed in her seat, smiled, and made light of the situation every time Gram made another move until he eventually got the picture.

Just as he had arrived there, Gram Parsons was being transported out of Altamont by chopper—a very different kind of chopper, but a chopper nonetheless. This one was filled with Rolling Stones, rock star hangers-on, groupies, and the promise of a brighter, more decadent, and thankfully wildly distracting future. As the chopper made its descent into San Francisco, Gram could see the road laying out in front of him, and finally his head stopped aching.

Altamont was one road, one distraction. Nellcôte was another road, another type of distraction entirely. Keith's rented mansion/makeshift recording studio along the French Riviera was a parade of darkness and debauchery, where the Rolling Stones were endeavoring to squeeze genre-bending music out of the cracks of the musty mansion's foundation. Gram watched as Keith stepped on the newest batch of Corsican-delivered heroin. Keith was shabby but surgical in his approach; hovering over his rented mansion's dining room table shirtless, wearing nothing but low-slung, striped corduroys, Keith carefully doled out the appropriate balance of quinine and then talcum powder and added it to the pile of pink Thai heroin.

After the Corsicans dropped off the first kilo, Gram suggested cutting the incredibly strong batch with laundry detergent. Unexperienced in most things in life compared to Keith Richards, Gram Parsons was overruled. This incredibly lethal heroin needed to be tempered, but he didn't want to turn it into a batch of street skag. Last year, while in the States, Keith had heard of a drug dealer in Harlem who had been flying in nearly pure heroin from Vietnam and distributing it at 12 percent potency compared to the usual 5 percent potency of most street dope. His trick was cutting the smack with quinine and mannite; nonintoxicating medication as opposed to cutting it like most dealers did with rat poison or, as Gram had suggested, with laundry detergent.

If they were going to make this kilo last a month, before the Corsicans zipped in again—up the French Riviera on their speedboats— then Keith and Gram needed to cut the smack properly. Quinine, yes. Talcum powder, maybe. Laundry detergent, definitely not.

Gram felt the sting of dejection but shrugged it off. He needed a fix. Getting a hair across his ass about it wasn't going to help matters. Satisfied that the heroin was properly calibrated, Keith dipped his switchblade into the pile, scooped out a sizable bump, turned to Gram, who was standing at his side nearly salivating. In a voice that was part laughter, part two-pack-a-day cough, he said, "Have at it, boy."

Gram delicately brought his nose to the blade, looked up to Keith dutifully, and with gratitude pressed his right thumb to his right nostril, vacuuming up the powder in one quick snort. The heroin shot through him like a comet. Hard, fast, and without regard for anything in its path. Gram stumbled a bit, groped about with his hands, rested them on the dining room table's surface, and hung his heavy head to his chest. His long, dark hair swung delicately as he tried steadying himself. He then gently slumped back into the chair behind him and nodded off. Keith laughed to himself, thinking, *Lightweight*, as he went back to work.

Gram awoke to the sounds of Keith and his bandmates messing with a slow blues from the studio in the cellar. Mick laid it on thick with the vocal:

Honey, I've been lying
Honey, I've been jiving
Honey, I've been signifying.

The tune quickly devolved. It was obvious that Keith had lost interest in whatever Diddley-esque hoodoo Mick was attempting to conjure.

Then Gram heard the newly familiar chords to Keith's latest masterpiece, "All Down the Line," burbling up from the basement into a blast of swampy sonic magnificence.

G—C—D—G. Keith carved out the riff with his Tele.

Charlie and Bill pulled the rhythm into form. Mick Taylor skidded across the top of it all with his loose slide while Jagger channeled Big Mama Thornton through his skinny English frame.

Yeah hear the women sighing, all down the line
Oh, hear the children crying, all down the line.

Keith then pushed the tune to the IV chord. Mick hit the chorus. He couldn't contain himself. He muscled over to Mick and sang out into Jagger's handheld mic alongside him. The two of them a shambolic mess of spontaneous rock 'n' roll brilliance; their voices saturated with junk and ambition, respectively:

Well you can't say yes, and you can't say no
Just be right there when the whistle blows.

Before jumping back into the riff, Keith let out a short, ecstatic "Yeah!"

Gram heard it all unfold from upstairs. He brimmed with jealousy. The basement—while the Stones were recording—was strictly off-limits unless you were contributing to the music in a meaningful way. And, well-meaning as he was, there was nothing meaningful about Gram's contribution to the Rolling Stones' recordings while exiled from British taxmen on the French Riviera in Keith Richards's rented mansion during the summer of 1971. Unless of course, you count being Keith Richards's junkie pilot fish as particularly meaningful to the long lasting greatness of what would become the Stones' masterpiece, *Exile on Main Street.*

No, during working hours—midnight-ish to whenever Keith passed out—Gram was relegated to the upstairs with the women and the rest of the junkie hangers-on.

It sucked.

Gram wanted more. He thought he had made progress with Keith. Progress toward what, he couldn't really say, but progress nonetheless. He and Keith would get high and sit around talking country music until the sun came up, trading songs.

"Have you heard this Jimmie Rodgers tune?"

"What about this Buck Owens record? I love Buck. Poor bloke is always the wronged man."

"What about the devil, in the weeds deep in those Louvin Brothers lyrics? Heavy."

Gram knew Keith liked him. Keith wanted him around, but he also knew Mick hated him. Hated the contention that someone else, someone like *Gram Parsons*, was going to teach him, *Mick Jagger*, about country music. Mick wrote "Dead Flowers" after all. Fuck you very much, Mr. Parsons.

Mick's distaste for him was obvious, but so what? Okay, so Gram wasn't going to join the Rolling Stones, still, maybe Keith would make good on his idea to have him produce Gram's solo record? Keith seemed into it but wouldn't commit.

Gram played it cool. He'd grab time with Keith when he could. And when he couldn't he'd keep working on that song he'd been messing with. He grabbed Keith's acoustic and headed upstairs for some quiet. Picking up the Gibson, he put words to the pain roiling within:

Time can pass and time can heal
But it don't ever pass the way I feel
You went away a long time ago
And why you left I never knew.

In those rare lucid moments at Villa Nellcôte, when not totally high on smack or fall-down drunk, Gram would keep his demons down by working on songs for his next musical project: a solo album. Gram wanted to do things his way. And do them unencumbered by the creative restrictions of bandmates. He had a vision. A vision of America through the lens of his own cosmic experiences and aspirations—*Cosmic American Music*—and he would bring it to life through a unique and unprecedented melding of the American country, soul, and gospel music he'd grown up in the South listening to, all expressed through the prism of pain he'd been enduring since his father's suicide. He kept writing.

But even songwriting had its hang-ups. No matter how he cut it, Gram kept running headfirst into his own despair. His own sadness. His unprocessed grief. It reared its beastly head everywhere. Writing songs in his head, up on the second floor of Keith's rented mansion was no exception.

When he couldn't write, he'd shoot heroin. When he couldn't shoot heroin, he'd write. Life was one long race to outrun the beast raging inside him. Daring him to look around the corner of his consciousness. To confront the pain inside him. For Gram Parsons, there was no peace.

Gram buoyed back and forth between complete inebriation and half-assed attempts at songwriting, all while marveling at the work ethic of Keith and his bandmates, who, no matter what drugs or drink were swimming through their systems, no matter what the situation or the environment, always seemed to rise to the creative challenge. Their approach to their craft—making the greatest rock 'n' roll music the world had ever heard, being the greatest rock 'n' roll band the world had ever seen, and doing it all without a playbook—was inspiring to Gram. And also totally intimidating.

For rock musicians in the early '70s—not just for Gram Parsons and the Rolling Stones, but for Eric Clapton, the Band, the Eagles, Bob Dylan, the Grateful Dead, John Lennon, George Harrison, and Elton John—the race was on to see who could crack the code to American roots music. A music with a fascinatingly rich stew of influences—Delta blues, country, soul, gospel, R&B. This mixture had produced the first generation of rock 'n' rollers that the Stones and their contemporaries had all grown up on and who had influenced them to start making music in the first place, artists like Elvis Presley, Jerry Lee Lewis, Bo Diddley, and others. How could this endlessly fascinating music, *American music*, be reimagined into something entirely new for today's generation of rock 'n' roll fans? That was the question.

For the Rolling Stones, this recording at Nellcôte was their opportunity to answer. It was their own, wholly unique and modern interpretation of America. The music the Stones were concocting in Keith's sweaty basement would shine a light on the underbelly of Americana and show the world the potential of where rock music as a genre could go. *Exile on Main Street*, the record they emerged with, was a masterpiece. It was official: the race was won, the Rolling Stones were kings, creative rock 'n' roll royalty, and Gram Parsons was nothing but a sidenote to the history they were writing. He was at best a junkie court jester hoping for a seat in Keith Richards's royal rock 'n' roll sidecar.

Gram needed to get his shit together and dry out or he'd be dead before he was thirty. So he split…for the desert.

Joshua Tree National Park is about a 140-mile drive from LA. It's located in a small desert town filled with entertainment industry burnouts, seekers, angel-dusted LSD heads, and UFO chasers. Gram Parsons was in one way or another, all of these things. After his experience at Nellcôte, Gram found his way to LA and burned his way through the Hollywood rock scene before landing out at Joshua Tree to clean up his act and earnestly start writing songs for what he hoped would become his first solo album.

Gram loved Joshua Tree, and why wouldn't he? It's a place unlike any other on the planet. Its desert is a psychedelics' acid dream come true with its trippy yucca trees, sun-blistered terrain, and glittering, star-freckled nighttime sky. And the town of Joshua Tree was and still is a low-key hippie outlaw's paradise. There's a lawless vibe about it. There aren't a lot of people, and most of those that live there seem to be trying to avoid some sort of hassle.

At night, Gram would head out to Joshua Tree National Park and frolic through the desert, high on acid and hoping to spot UFOs and/or God. Both were pursuits he believed in: Gram, the onetime Ivy Leaguer now cosmic country musician, used God to get into Harvard University. His grades weren't that good in high school, but he wrote an essay on God in his application that blew the board away. His family's money might have also blown them away.

During the day in Joshua Tree, Gram would sleep off the

Gram Parsons praying at the altar of Keith Richards…and heroin.

LSD and try to write songs from the cozy confines of his room at the Joshua Tree Inn. Not exactly clean living, but at least he wasn't doing heroin. However, getting fucked-up and tripping balls eventually won out, and Gram's writing took a back seat. So be it, he thought. Being high kept the pain away. He'd get around to writing and to making his solo record in due time.

Meanwhile, *Exile on Main Street* was a smash. Gram was happy for his old friend Keith, but a part of him was pissed off that he wasn't along for the ride. He couldn't help but think that all that country music he'd shared with Keith had helped inform the sound of *Exile*. Now, the record was double platinum, and what did Gram have to show for it other than an increasingly intense heroin addiction?

But what had Gram even more upset was a new band that was quickly becoming unavoidable on the FM dial. The Eagles featured Gram's ex-bandmate from the Burrito Brothers, Bernie Leadon, and it represented everything Gram hated about modern rock 'n' roll, to say nothing of his annoyance at their infusing country into their brand of rock and effectively working his side of the street. The Eagles traded on all of the country and none of the soul influences that Gram had been messing with since he started making music back at Harvard with the International Submarine Band, then through his work with the Byrds and ultimately to his near-perfect first album with the Flying Burrito Brothers. Gram had dedicated his life to fusing country and soul into a new form of rock 'n' roll, and here was this new band of assholes who— judging from the high-gloss production of their singles—cared little for the actual spirit of this music and only for the success that its most watered-down, trite realization could bring. "Peaceful Easy Feeling"? More like a "plastic dry fuck," went Gram's assessment.

Gram Parsons *hated* the Eagles.

Gram knew he could do better. It was time. Time to get out of the desert. Time to put a studio band together. Time to get some songs going and make this damn album and time to deal with his damn demons. To do that, Gram needed to get in touch with his road manager and friend, Phil Kaufman.

By 1972, Phil Kaufman was already an outsized character in LA rock 'n' roll lore. He was a rock star's fixer. Whatever you needed, he'd procure. Whatever you didn't need, he'd make disappear. That sort of thing. He'd worked for the Stones, Bob Dylan, and the Band.

But Kaufman's mystique amongst LA music industry illuminati came not from his road manager experience but from his days spent with Charles Manson, running girls for petty thefts and sexcapades. Kaufman had once shared a cell with Manson while jailed at Terminal Island on a drug bust. When he bounced, Kaufman needed a place to stay, so he took up with Charlie and his girls. He fell in quick with the Manson family. It was all the sex and acid he could handle. But it proved to be too much, and Phil eventually split. When the Tate-LaBianca murders happened, and Phil watched as Charlie's girls were paraded across the television in 1971, he remarked to himself that he'd "had sex with every one of those murderesses."

He came on professionally at first with Gram as a sort of road manager and minder, but the two quickly established a legit friendship. Phil saw it as his duty to take care of the fragile singer-songwriter. He made sure Gram didn't take too much smack, didn't sleep with the wrong women, and made it to the gig or the studio on time.

When Phil got the call, he hightailed it out to Joshua Tree, grabbed Gram, brought him back to LA, and nestled him into an apartment at the Chateau Marmont. At first, Gram was motivated. Inspired and ready to get down to work. The two made travel arrangements for Gram's new muse, Emmylou Harris, the beautiful singer with the enchanting voice whom Gram had met on the road. Then they got Barry Tashian, the former singer of the Remains, to fly in from Nashville and immediately begin working on a repertoire for Gram. Barry brought with him a suitcase of songs: "Streets of Baltimore" by Harlan Howard and Tompall Glaser, "I Can't Dance" by Tom T. Hall, and "Cry One More Time" by Peter Wolf and Seth Justman of the J. Geils Band, a white-hot R&B band from back in Tashian's home turf in Boston, Massachusetts.

With these songs, along with the handful of originals he'd been working up, Gram could see his album taking shape.

But working on original material brought painful emotions to the surface, and Gram quickly fell into the familiar habit of burying the pain with alcohol and heroin. Gram was incoherent for long stretches of time. More of a rambling buffoon than a tender troubadour. Kaufman and Tashian knew that making this record wasn't going to be easy. They needed to act quick while Gram had some semblance of motivation and before he was completely consumed by his addiction, so naturally they headed to Sin City to find a band.

The trip to Las Vegas was strictly business. Tashian and Gram had a job to do: convince Elvis Presley's band to back Gram in the studio for his new record. It was a brilliant idea. While the rest of the rock 'n' roll world was busy chasing country music up the charts, putting their hair in ponytails, and fitting themselves for snap-buttoned shirts and bolo ties, all the while paying scant attention to the soul and spirit at the heart of country music, Gram decided to hire deeply talented musicians who got this music on a molecular level. And the fact that they were seen at the time as being tragically unhip, backing Elvis as a show band in Vegas, running through a career retrospective of square cheese for beehived housewives and black-framed pencil necks in for the early bird special on junkets from the Midwest, made the move by Gram all the more ingenious. While self-satisfied country rock 'n' rollers like the Eagles fiddled with learning Chet Atkins and Floyd Cramer riffs on guitar and piano, Gram would have James Burton and Glen D. Hardin playing guitar and piano *in his studio band.* Two players who could both come out on your porch or step into your parlor and show you how it all went down.

Hiring Elvis's band paid off, big time. In addition to having stone-cold killers in the studio, Gram, with so much respect for these musicians, kept himself sober through the work. The result was stunning. The sessions with Elvis's band produced a masterpiece. The record—*GP*, as it would come to be called—was Gram Parsons's vision of Cosmic American Music come to life: a perfect meld of country, soul, and gospel; Southern gothic tradition and irony and inner pain channeled through bent Telecaster strings, R&B chord progressions, and honky tonk piano riffs.

Gram's heavy, soft-spoken, understated singing voice stank of heroin. He sang loose and slack-jawed, but his admiration for Conway Twitty lent a measure of directness to the vocals, and the mix of those ingredients manifested an emotional harpoon of vulnerability that cut straight through to the hearts of listeners.

GP is a staggering work of artistry, and the boys in Elvis's band couldn't help but wonder what a record might sound like if their other front man, the one with the sideburns and ever-expanding waistline, was given the artistic freedom to make the records he wanted to make. But they knew that would never happen. The Colonel had too many Vegas seats to fill and too many early bird specials to shill.

When the record was completed, Gram was emotionally spent. So he headed out to Joshua Tree to chase UFOs again.

But there would be little rest for Gram Parsons and his damaged soul in 1973. Grief would soon roar back into his life. On July 15, 1973, Gram's friend and frequent musical collaborator, the great guitarist and onetime Byrd Clarence White, was struck by a drunk driver while loading gear into his car after a gig. He died instantly. When Gram heard the news, he was besieged by grief.

Though overpopulated by long-haired musicians, the funeral for White was a staid, Catholic affair. The opposite of what Gram thought his friend would have wanted. During the graveside portion of the service, Gram took it upon himself to pay an honest tribute to White. Unprompted by any family member of White's or by any funeral or church official of any capacity, Gram launched into song at his friend's grave and in front of scores of grieving musicians. The gesture brought some level of catharsis to those in attendance, more than anything the priest had said, anyway. Gram understood grief. Grief was hardwired to his soul. The beast in Gram knew well and good when to rouse itself, and this was one occasion where its presence was welcomed.

But after the funeral, Gram drowned the beast in alcohol at a local bar filled with friends. Among them was his now-ubiquitous sidekick, Phil Kaufman. It was there that Gram and Phil made a pact to one another, that no matter who kicked first, the other would make sure that under no circumstance would the dearly departed among them be sent off in the soulless fashion foisted upon their soulful friend, Clarence White. "Fuck that straight-laced funeral jive," Gram said. "Take me out to the desert in Joshua Tree, burn my body up, and set my soul free." A handshake and two shots of well tequila with cold Schlitz chasers sealed it.

Gene Hackman was pissed. Learning your lines was hard enough. Getting into character emotionally was another thing entirely. The fucking distractions on a movie set were monumental to begin with but now, with cops busting up his scene to arrest the biker who owned the house they'd arranged to shoot this scene in, the entire day would be shot to shit. Gene would never be able to get back into character now.

Hackman and director Arthur Penn watched with a mix of incredulity and annoyance as the owner of the house, Phil Kaufman, was led out under the lowering boom and through the film crew in handcuffs. The whispers started immediately:

"Kaufman burned the body."

"The one the newspapers had been talking about for the past couple days."

"The body in the desert. That junkie country singer…"

The newspapers had it right. Kaufman did burn the body and he didn't care who knew about it and he'd do it again if he had to to make sure that his friend, Gram Parsons, was honored in death that way that he had pledged to do for him in life.

After Clarence White's funeral, Gram Parsons was focused. When *GP* failed to set the world on fire, Gram was disappointed but undeterred. He was hell-bent on making another great record.

Gram Parsons: Cosmic American poet, Keith Richards's pilot fish, and chaser of UFOs.

But first Gram needed some rest. He headed back to Joshua Tree for some R&R. He was happy. He had a strong feeling that when this new, yet-to-be-written album was released, the results would be different. The world would finally get hip to Gram Parsons and his Cosmic American Music. Hell, at least the local bar out at Joshua Tree had one of his songs on the jukebox. He made it a point to hang out as much as possible at his new local and to hit the stage whenever the mood struck him. One night, while sitting in with a local band and working their way through Merle Haggard's "Okie from Muskogee," Gram took note of how the pedal steel player couldn't keep up with the rest. When they finished the set, Gram found out why. The steel player's arms were loaded with track marks from shooting junk and were so badly bruised he could barely move them, never mind play steel.

The sight of the track marks wet Gram's whistle. He'd been drinking most of the day and night and taking pills, but now he had heroin on his brain. That familiar junkie jones kicked in. Subconsciously he knew that no amount of booze, pills, or promise of the future would stave off the pain for too long. Heroin, though? Heroin took it all away.

So Gram and a couple friends he was traveling with split. They knew they could fix back at the hotel. Back at the Joshua Tree Inn a local heroin dealer was arranged for Gram. When the dealer arrived, she had her two-year-old with her. Gram didn't mind. But he did mind that the dealer didn't come as advertised. She didn't actually have any heroin. Instead, she had vials of stolen government-grade morphine sulfate. At this point, Gram didn't care. He could feel the saliva dripping down the inner walls of his cheeks. He could feel the giddy pitter-patter of his heart picking up speed in anticipation of getting high. He needed to feel the rush of opiates blast up his veins and wipe away the coming hurt. Morphine was close enough and it would have to do. Gram would just take twice as much.

So he did.

And immediately things went south. Gram's overdose came quick. His breathing slowed. Then it grew rasped. His two friends managed to get him up and into the tub with his clothes off. They jammed ice cubes into his asshole, a home remedy almost as old as ice itself, which shocked his system and revived him. Gram was mumbling and semiconscious, but within no time the morphine once again took control of his faculties. No frozen enemas would be able to help him this time. And then, Gram felt next to nothing. Just warm bliss. His body went slack. His mind went black. No pain.

Gram Parsons overdosed and died in room 8 of the Joshua Tree Inn on September 19, 1973.

When Phil Kaufman heard the news, he was back in LA and he was pissed. Pissed that Gram had been so careless. Pissed that Gram's traveling friends hadn't known how to keep him alive, and pissed that he wasn't there to take care of his friend himself.

He wouldn't let that happen again.

The friend in Joshua Tree who'd called Kaufman to give him the news mentioned that authorities were taking his body away. So he moved fast. He made it to the Joshua Tree Inn from LA in three hours. Kaufman immediately cleaned out Gram's room, wiping away any trace of an illicit drug party. He then rounded up Gram's two friends and got them out of Joshua Tree and back to LA where they would be beyond the reach of the local police and therefore unable to be questioned. Kaufman knew how to clean up a rock 'n' roll mess.

But the job wasn't done.

Once back in LA, Kaufman called the Joshua Tree morgue to inquire about his friend's body. Gram's family, upon hearing of his death in the press, had made arrangements for it to be flown back home to New Orleans. The body was chilling in an airport hangar at LAX, waiting to be retrieved by Gram's stepfather for what would no doubt be a stale, religious, conservative Southern funeral service. In other words, the exact opposite of what Gram would want.

Kaufman, ever the fixer, had a friend who owned a hearse. He borrowed it, grabbed some other friends—a motley crew of leather-clad, greasy-haired rock 'n' roll biker types who Kaufman knew could serve as impromptu illicit pallbearers—and then headed out to LAX. On the way they pounded bottles of Mickey's wide-mouth grenades and shared pints of Beam, Cuervo, and Jack.

Kaufman wheeled the hearse to the off-ramp toward LAX and straight toward the shipping hangar. He and his band of rock 'n' roll pallbearers bounded out of the car and headed into the office area. The square behind the desk was either scared, stupid, or both, because he bought the long line of crap Kaufman fed him: They were off-duty funeral home workers there to move the body by private plane.

Unbelievably, Kaufman was given clearance to grab the coffin. So he did. And he and his cohorts began wheeling it out of the hangar to their waiting hearse. Just then a cop in a black-and-white on patrol pulled up to see what in the hell was going on with what must have looked to him like a drunken gang of biker body snatchers.

Kaufman was quick with the bullshit.

"Officer! You're just in time. We're a man short and not sure how we're going to get the coffin into the back of our hearse. Can you give us a hand?"

Remarkably and without question, the officer did just that.

Gram Parsons's body was snatched.

Next stop? Joshua Tree.

But first they needed gas. So, once out of LA and well on their way to the desert, they stopped off at a gas station and filled five gallons. Kaufman and his men drank the entire ride out. They were wasted by the time they made it out to Joshua Tree National Park. The area of the desert that Gram loved so much. The part of the world that allowed him to run free of his pain, to chase UFOs and to leave all the grief behind.

At around 1:00 a.m., the hearse made it out to the part of the desert known as Cap Rock and stopped. The stars were electric. It was a beautiful night. Kaufman unfolded his drunken, greasy-jean-clad legs to the desert floor and walked around back. With his crew, he pulled Gram's wooden casket from the back of the hearse and dropped it unceremoniously onto the desert floor. Kaufman popped open the lid. There was Gram. Naked, dead, and bloated. Surgical tape covering the autopsy wounds.

Kaufman wasted no time. He grabbed the gallons of gasoline and poured it all over Gram's body. He lit a match. Dropped it and BOOM! Gram's body ignited into a fireball. His soul exploded into eternity in an overstated blast. It was so unlike him. Gram Parsons was subtle. He was marked by deep emotional pain and engaged in a quiet but constant race to outrun his grief. Regardless of the manner in which Gram Parsons's body left this world, there was no mistaking it—he was now free.

Phil's friend Gram was liberated. His other friend, Charlie Manson, was behind bars. His former bosses, the Rolling Stones, had established themselves as the "world's greatest rock 'n' roll band" and Phil Kaufman was sitting in his car, now an old man, a mangled shell of himself from back in those hazy days of lawless rock 'n' roll. Gram was on his mind lately because Gram was on the minds of lots of people lately. Gram Parsons and the myth that Kaufman helped create was going through a resurgence of popularity among a new generation of snap-buttoned, pony-tailed, country rock 'n' rollers. Sure, they added the prefix *alt* to *country*, but still, if it walks like an Eagle and sings like an Eagle it's probably a second-rate version of an Eagle, and that means it's a third-rate version of Gram Parsons.

CHAPTER 5

AXL ROSE

AXL ROSE FELT AT HOME on St. Mark's Place in Manhattan's East Village. He could feel the inspiration that drove his heroes, the Ramones and the New York Dolls, to create some of the most intense music he'd ever heard. Music that to this day—February 2, 1988—still spoke to the angry young man in him. Squalor, crime, and grime. Punk rockers, skinheads, and hippies hanging on for dear life. Homeless people, drag queens, junkies, and tourists. St. Mark's was a low-key bohemian bazaar of countercultures clashing up against one another in the form of hard-to-find books, harder-to-find records, and imported porn. Studded belts, Dr. Martens boots, leather for days, and other edgy, irreverent fashion items unavailable to the rest of America like that CHARLIE DON'T SURF T-shirt hanging in the window of Trash and Vaudeville. The one with Manson's 1969 mugshot—big and intense—emblazoned across the front. Axl thought it was killer, so he popped into the store and had the dude with the peroxide hair and Iggy Pop tattoo behind the counter grab it for him. Axl wouldn't wear it onstage that night, though. No, he had his Thin Lizzy shirt teed up for that.

The show, later that evening at the Ritz, a couple blocks north of St. Mark's, was being broadcast live on MTV, and Axl's band, Guns N' Roses was wired tight for maximum rock 'n' roll. America took notice. When it aired, the show was watched by a relatively small audience of American teenagers, up way past their bedtimes. But the show was recorded on dusty VHS tapes and passed around high school corridors repeatedly over the coming months until the ferocity of Guns N' Roses was recognized and salivated over en masse by high school kids everywhere.

Axl Rose came to life onscreen as a real-life version of *The Breakfast Club*'s Johnny Bender. He was the high school burnout who we all knew growing up. The one who doubled down on shop electives and wore ripped jeans out of necessity, not out of a sense of fashion. The guy who sported self-imposed cigarette burns on his muscular forearms and was rumored to have a Bud Man tattoo on his ass. This was the same dude who sat in the back of the classroom and simultaneously frightened and attracted the cheerleaders. Those same cheerleaders who wouldn't give *you* the time of day. You saw this dude standing alone—quiet—at the edge of the keg party up off the train tracks. You left him alone because you heard the story about the time he busted the bottle of Michelob across the jock with the big mouth's face, but inside you burned to know more about him. What made him tick? What made him so pissed? What made him so fucking *cool*?

Just like that kid, Axl was filled with contempt and untapped confidence. Onstage at the Ritz, you could feel his anger. It was something that had been building up inside since birth. It was coming out one way or another. Likely through violent rage or petty crime or both. But rock 'n' roll saves. Otherwise Axl Rose would likely have been in jail on that night instead of blowing the minds of all in attendance as well as everyone watching at home on television and later on Memorex.

Onstage, Axl looked a little older than the millions of high school burnouts who would soon come to worship him and his band. He was essentially the same angry young man he was growing up back in Lafayette, Indiana, but at the Ritz, it was clear that his time had come. And he'd arrived with a murderer's row of bandmates: Slash, the bronzed Mad Hatter Adonis; Izzy Stradlin with his "Ronnie Wood via Johnny Thunders" cool; Duff McKagan, eleven feet tall and oozing punk rock sex and excitement; and last, the wide-eyed ball of heavy metal puppy dog charisma, Steven Adler. A band that you could immediately tell never had a fuck to give. And their live show was flawless—even with the flaws, it was flawless. Songs like the Diddley-esque "Mr. Brownstone," the jet-fueled "Nightrain," and the showstopper "Rocket Queen" veer from brilliant to trainwreck and back again in the time it takes to suck a Marlboro red from first flame down to toxic filter.

GNR was from the street and for the street. Their lyrics represented a band living a hand-to-mouth life of rock 'n' roll debauchery and all too willing to let themselves die in the pursuit of it. You couldn't tell if they were creatively brave—risking it all in the service of making totally authentic rock 'n' roll—or if they were just too stupid to know any better. Through it all, the band was impossibly cool. Every shot. Every pose. Every note (even the out-of-tune ones from Slash), every vocal (even the ones from Axl that run out of breath), all combined to somehow make them seem even cooler. If you tried, you couldn't have created a more representative version of a rock 'n' roll band than the one Axl Rose took to the Ritz stage on February 2, 1988. You wouldn't know it from watching them, but that band, and the fuck-all attitude that propelled it, and more specifically its singer, had been a long time in the making.

Young Axl Rose, juvenile delinquent.

The crack from the back of the hand to his mouth came quick. It was unexpected. And it stung like a motherfucker. Young Axl could taste his blood bubbling up from his lip. The damage could have been worse, but luckily Axl's dad didn't wear rings. Jewelry was too ostentatious for a Pentecostal. So was Barry Manilow and his No. 1 hit, "Mandy," which was what put Axl on the receiving end of another blow to the grill. Axl made the mistake of absent-mindedly singing along to the song's chorus with its lyrics that his dad somehow considered sexually suggestive. Axl seriously did not understand how he was related to this dude, his old man, this abusive, religious nutbag. But that was because Axl wasn't actually related to him. He just didn't know it yet. Then again, young Axl Rose didn't know much beyond Led Zeppelin riffs, Elton John melodies, and pent-up rage for the man he thought was his father.

Soon, young Axl would learn that his father was really his step-father and that his real father was *never* to be brought up. It was a discovery that did little to endear Axl to his stepdad, and thus the violence continued. It wasn't reserved for just Axl, either. His stepdad threw his fists around to keep Axl's mom in line as well. Axl saw it all as a little boy and a teenager: the beatings and the mental anguish.

By the time he was sixteen, rock 'n' roll was his only salvation. That and his new friend Izzy. They vibed on the Stones, AC/DC, Aerosmith, and the new onslaught of British punk bands invading America: the Sex Pistols, Generation X, and the Clash.

They also bonded over beer, grass, and pills. And of course, the two of them, especially Axl, took every opportunity possible to fuck with the local authorities. Axl had a real hatred for the small-town, conservative, square-jawed local cops. To him, they were just an extension of the repression and bullshit rules imposed by his stepdad, except out on the street he could talk back and let loose the inner rage he carried. An arrest for disturbing the peace was worth it. He could never let loose on his stepdad like he could on the cops. Plus, the cops would have to catch him first. So Axl mouthed off to Lafayette's Finest every chance he got, and the cops, in turn, found a special kind of satisfaction whenever they could bust his ass and throw him in jail. The result was a long string of juvenile arrests for petty crimes, public drunkenness, loitering, etc.

Fucking with the cops was always fun, but music was becoming the main focus for Axl. And for Izzy. They put a little band together and played when they could, but mostly they studied and listened to the masters whenever they got the chance.

Their latest obsession was the soundtrack album from the film *Over the Edge*, an adolescent crime drama set in the fictional suburb of "Granada" where the town's kids, bored and tired of being neglected by their parents and other authority figures finally rebel, setting about to destroy and terrorize their town through a fiery crime spree. He could relate to the teenage wasteland/anti-authority vibe it portrayed. Just like the kids in Granada, Axl felt neglected, ignored, and oppressed, and was compelled to vent his unhappiness through violence. Plus, the movie's soundtrack was the shit: Cheap Trick, Van Halen, the Cars, Jimi Hendrix, and even that ballad at the end, the one by Valerie Carter that played while the kids were bused off to juvenile hall—it was all right up Axl's alley.

But Axl wouldn't be shipped off to juvie. He'd soon be on a bus headed for a different kind of jungle altogether: Los Angeles, California.

In the mid-1980s, on the side of Los Angeles where a mile-and-a-half stretch of Sunset Boulevard curves through West Hollywood and is known as "the Strip" or "Sunset Strip," a new kind of heavy metal was doing everything it could to put LA on the musical map: glam metal.

Glam metal took its musical cues from British glam rock; the sounds of bands like Sweet, Slade, T-Rex, and Mott the Hoople traded on big, crunchy guitar riffs, deep-pocket grooves, sex-laden vocals, and hedonistic lyrics. British glam rock was a sophisticated kind of cool that owed much to David Bowie and Queen, but its American offshoot, glam *metal*, kept one foot planted in the concrete jungles of Iggy Pop and Alice Cooper while peacocking through the glitzed streets of Los Angeles. Fashion threaded the two styles together, but the U.S. version was more masculine, tougher, and a touch violent. LA glam bands like Mötley Crüe would meld the androgyny of Marc Bolan with the apocalyptic look of Mad Max. The result was something wildly unique and somehow representative of the violence tearing through the streets of Los Angeles at the time.

In 1985 violent crime in LA exploded to unprecedented levels due to the city's heavy trafficking of crack cocaine. You couldn't avoid the headlines if you tried, but glam metalheads did their best to ignore the harsh reality enveloping their city by setting up their own bacchanalia on Sunset, where every night they drank, drugged, and fucked away their worries to the sounds of the Strip's hottest bands at the time: W.A.S.P., Ratt, Poison, and the aforementioned

Mötley Crüe. There was no mistaking what LA's new music scene was all about: debauchery. And their fans loved it. They showed up every night en masse, packing clubs like the Starwood and the Whisky a Go Go to get a glimpse of the hedonism up close and personal. Glam music was an escape from reality, unlike the music being made on the other end of town.

Down in South Central Los Angeles, where the effects of the crack epidemic were being felt most severely, rap music—up until that point mostly an East Coast export—was taking on a new identity, one that mirrored the harsh circumstances of Los Angeles street life. It would come to be known as "gangsta rap," and where LA's glam ran from reality, LA's gangsta rap ran straight toward it and smacked it in its mouth with the butt of a Glock.

In Compton, about twenty miles south of the Strip in Hollywood, a local drug dealer named Eric Wright watched his cousin get shot and killed over a drug beef and decided it was time to find a new job. He took the quarter million in cash he had stashed from selling coke and invested it into the formation of a new record label with a music promoter named Jerry Heller. They called the label Ruthless Records, and Eric started calling himself "Eazy-E." After releasing a record under his own name, Eazy formed the group N.W.A. with producer and rapper Dr. Dre, Ice Cube, MC Ren, and DJ Yella. N.W.A., along with the rapper Ice-T, would force America to pay attention to their neighborhoods that were being destroyed by drugs and violence. Streets where their neighbors clashed violently with police, who were supposedly there to protect them, frequently and oftentimes to deadly ends.

The beats these LA rappers made were bigger than anything from the East Coast and the lyrics they spat out were more direct, honest, and profane than anything anyone had heard in music before, anywhere.

And Axl Rose loved it. All of it. Mid-1980s LA music was as fraught with tension and manic energy as he was. It was bipolar. On one end, a low-down slap of unforgiving reality; a gut punch to authority. And on the other end, a high-flying, endless party; distraction via debauchery. He could appreciate the scene up on Sunset, but in his heart he knew that there wasn't one band among them who could fuck with what he and his new bandmates were about to bring to the party.

Once Axl Rose arrived in Hollywood from Lafayette, Indiana, the transformation from small-town delinquent to streetwalking chee-tah was quick. After a few false starts and along with his hometown bud, Izzy, Axl formed Guns N' Roses.

Out on the streets and in the clubs, the band quickly developed a reputation as the nastiest hard rock 'n' roll band on the Sunset Strip. Let those other LA bands call themselves "glam." Guns, or "GNR," was going to stand out in the scene by separating themselves from the scene. They weren't "glam," they were "hard." And they weren't "metal," they were "rock." Hard rock. A simple but novel distinction to bring to the stage on the Strip. And offstage, Axl, Izzy, and their

Axl Rose, product of Los Angeles.

new bandmates, Slash, Duff, and Steven, lived the life authentically: They drank and drugged harder than Mötley Crüe. They fucked more strippers than Poison. They got into it with the LA County Sheriff's Department whenever they could and were quick to brawl with posers, yuppies, squares, or whoever else got in their faces. They were the real deal.

And their songs were *great*. Totally authentic, and as such the band's appeal was undeniable. They packed them in at the Troubadour, the Starwood, and the Whisky. In 1986 GNR signed to Geffen Records, despite fears from executives that the band would be dead before their record was even released. The thinking among Geffen employees was that if the drink and drugs didn't get them, then they'd self-destruct via Axl's wild temper.

The band was generally a mess. They were basically homeless. Guns N' Roses squatted in their rehearsal space. A one-car-sized storage unit off Sunset Boulevard behind the Sunset Grill. They slept among their gear. There was no kitchen and no bathroom. But there was a constant party. When not rehearsing, which they did constantly, they'd get high and get drunk on Nightrain with the whores from down on Hollywood Boulevard, and party with members of Faster Pussycat, Redd Kross, and Thelonious Monster.

Soon young kids from the Valley started showing up to listen to the band rehearse. Steven and Slash would play nice for a bit and scam them out of their money under the guise of procuring drugs for them. Axl didn't have time for such pretenses. He would just roll them for whatever cash he could get. Young women— valley girls and prostitutes alike—were subjected to a "Get Naked or Leave" policy. The fucking would spill out into the alley, and while little suburban valley boys realized their fantasies and got with the professionals from Hollywood and Vine, the guys in the band would empty their pants pockets for their cash and clean out the purses of the less-suspecting prostitutes.

Word on the strip spread: There was a party going on. And it was wild.

One time, Don Henley from the Eagles showed up. Impressed and horrified by the debauchery, Henley was moved to write "Sunset Grill," a song he would include on his second solo album:

You see a lot more meanness in the city
It's the kind that eats you up inside
Hard to come away with anything that feels like dignity.

Their party grew. The band was sounding great but still wasn't making any money, so Izzy started slinging dope to bring in cash. People were talking; Guns N' Roses were fucking nuts and their parties were awesome, plus they had great heroin. Eventually, even Izzy's hero, Aerosmith guitarist Joe Perry, showed up to score.

There were too many scantily clad spandex prostitutes and groupies to count, and telling them apart from one another was becoming a real problem for Slash. When it came to women, Slash was largely indiscriminate, but he did like the good girls; they usually had apartments he could crash at, and those apartments had running water and toilets.

The party raged, and soon enough the West Hollywood sheriff's deputies started coming around to restore order. Axl would give 'em lip, and the next thing you knew, he'd be bent over, face smashed sideways on the hood of a cruiser, his wrists cuffed behind him. They'd either haul him in or smack him around or sometimes both. It was just like the old days in Lafayette. Nothing had really changed, and why should it have? Axl was no less pissed off.

Violence followed the band wherever it went. Bar fights, alley fights; they were the rule, not the exception. Even jumping off the stage midset to crack a wiseacre in the grill was fast becoming just part of the gig for members of GNR with Axl at the helm. The band took no shit.

Ever.

On July 21, 1987, the band's debut album, *Appetite for Destruction,* was released. Their star started to slowly rise, but growing fame didn't curtail the band's behavior. It only intensified it. Newfound celebrity and notoriety started to create a sense of isolation for Axl. A feeling that his lyrics for "Out ta Get Me" were a self-fulfilling prophecy:

> *Sometimes it's easy to forget where you're goin'*
> *Sometimes it's harder to leave*
> *And every time you think you know just what you're doin'*
> *That's when your troubles exceed.*

Axl wrote it mainly about Lafayette, but increasingly it seemed to be about the people around him now. Wherever he went, he believed, they were trying to keep him down. Just like authority figures back home, nowadays the cops, the record label, the promoters, and increasingly the press were trying to bleed out of him what it was that made him special in the first place. To get him to tone it down. To conform to their bullshit.

It was making him paranoid. And causing very dramatic mood swings. The mood swings were always there, but when the band was starting out, they'd derail a rehearsal or a party. Maybe a show. But as the band grew, so did the stakes, and mood swings at this stage of Axl's career were much harder for everyone to deal with.

In February 1988, just after their triumphant show at the Ritz in NYC, Guns N' Roses embarked on their first headlining tour. It was a big deal. And Axl was a big mess. He was jankier than usual and emotionally volatile. Some believed it was because of his relationship with girlfriend Erin Everly (daughter of rock 'n' roll royalty, Don Everly, one half of rock 'n' roll pioneers the Everly Brothers), but it was more likely that Axl's intensity was simply increasing in proportion to the growing stature of his band.

On February 12, for unspecified reasons, Axl blew off one of the band's first headlining shows in Phoenix, Arizona. He went missing. No one knew where he was. The second show in Phoenix, the next night, was also canceled. The band was immediately bounced by promoters from an upcoming opening slot on the highly coveted David Lee Roth tour. Further, they were eliminated from consideration for the opening slot on the even more highly coveted Jimmy Page tour. Opportunities that would have exposed them to larger audiences. Axl's bandmates were incensed. You don't pull a no-show. Not in the music business. It's a death sentence. A career killer. They contemplated kicking Axl out of the band for the offense. He had little contrition and less in the way of an excuse. He simply didn't show. And he simply didn't care if they wanted to kick him out of the band. Go ahead, he told them. Who are you going to get to replace me? He knew his place in the band was secure, but not without one major concession. Axl had to agree with his band, management, and label to undergo a psychiatric evaluation.

Axl submitted to tests at UCLA Medical Center. The doctors, in their evaluation, considered not only Axl's present state of almost constant emotional volatility but also the oppressive childhood that he detailed for them along with his twenty arrests. He presented a clinical diagnosis of manic-depressive disease, or what is commonly referred to today as bipolar disorder.

It made sense to Axl. And the prescribed lithium helped at times, but there was little he could do to completely quell the beast within. The mood swings continued. Bandmates weren't the only ones subjected to them. Fans and civilians weren't immune from the swings in mood that would sometimes escalate to full-on violent outbursts.

Axl beat a businessman senseless in a hotel bar for calling him a "Bon Jovi look-alike."

He nearly baited eighteen thousand fans into a full-scale riot at the Philadelphia Spectrum, fighting with the local cops patrolling the crowd because he thought they were harassing him before the show.

He was arrested for cracking his female neighbor over the head with a wine bottle because she complained about the noise.

The press took note. And bad press began popping up. So Axl added the media to his shit list. Second to the cops and third to his fucked-up stepdad, but prominently placed nonetheless. But nothing did more to undermine Axl Rose's already low opinion of the press than the reaction to the events that took place during Guns N' Roses' set at the Donington Monsters of Rock festival.

Anticipation for GNR's performance was peaked. Security was lax. Capacity was maxed. One hundred thousand rain-soaked bodies standing in the mud. Most of them drunk. The sun was buried behind dark, ominous clouds. The band knew something was wrong and began their set with trepidation. It mattered little. The crowd went apeshit. Barely into their second song, the audience lurched forward as one giant wave. Then a hole in the middle of the crowd opened up. Within seconds, bodies were sucked into an undertow of humanity. A massive mosh pit began. Izzy freaked out and stopped playing. The rest of the band followed suit. Axl tried his best from the front of the stage to chill the crowd out. Bodies began to be pulled out of the muddy melee, injured and in need of medical attention but alive. Once it looked as though order had been restored, the band kicked back into their set with "Paradise City," and shit got real. The crowd's moshing became violent and relentless. Thousands and thousands of people were worked into a fit, slamming wildly into each other to the sounds of the most dangerous band on the planet. The crowd swayed uncontrollably as one, and with a single false move it could overtake the stage or collapse in on itself at any moment. The band was frightened. They tried cooling things down with a new acoustic number, "Patience," and then gave it one more shot with "Sweet Child o' Mine," but it was no use. The crowd was too intense. Too terrifying. After the tune, the band bailed. Axl spat into the mic before leaving the stage, "Have a great fucking day and try not to fucking kill yourselves."

Little did he know, a few of them had already been killed. Later that night, in the hotel bar, the band was told that two of their fans at Donington had died. Trampled underfoot during their set. Both were so mangled they needed to be identified by the papers in their pockets and the tattoos on their bodies.

The press blamed the band. The story being printed and reprinted over and over was that GNR refused to stop playing despite the obvious danger in the air. Of course, Axl had stopped the show twice and eventually cut the entire set short. This was never reported. There was no advantage to the truth for the press. The story sold better if the dangerous junkies from Sunset Strip caught the blame.

None of this was lost on Axl. The deaths at Donington by themselves were hard enough to swallow. These were kids. Fans. And now they were dead and the press was blaming the band.

TWO DEAD AT DONINGTON, screamed the headlines. That was one more than Altamont.

His rage intensified. It seemed that whatever he did, authorities were out to get him. And the notoriety caused the band's popularity to grow. And the more his own fame and celebrity grew, the more shit he seemed to have to take from the press, from the cops, from whoever.

He tried retreating into himself, but by now MTV had begun playing the band's videos in heavy rotation, and their popularity skyrocketed. A new album was needed quickly to capitalize on their success, but a proper full length was impossible to put together with the band's touring schedule (not to mention the near-debilitating heroin habits of Izzy, Slash, and Steven and the general growing dysfunction of the band as a unit). So it was decided that an EP called *G N' R Lies* would be released as a stopgap. The concept was tabloid trash, a world that the band was becoming all too familiar with. The artwork was a *National Enquirer*–like cover that poked fun at the press and its growing fascination with the band. The music was a mix of covers and unreleased old and new tunes that the band had been working up live.

To Axl, *G N' R Lies* scanned the world of celebrity decadence and tawdry gossip against a tough-talking, hard-living, unseen street reality. As a record, it was bipolar. Like his LA. Like him.

Axl saw himself as a voice for this reality. Just as he believed Eazy-E saw himself as a voice for his reality. So he was going to spare none of the details and none of the reality he'd come to learn and to live around in Los Angeles. On the song "One in a Million" he sang out:

Police and niggers, that's right
Get outta my way.

When you first hear the N-word in the lyrics, there is a split second where your brain stops listening and you involuntarily ask yourself, "Did he *really* just say that?" and then, as if to answer your internal monologue, Axl immediately follows up the N-word with, "that's right" as in, "Yeah, motherfucker. I just said that. So what?"

Understandably, the press lost its collective mind. Axl was quickly labeled a racist as well as a homophobe for the following lyric, also from "One in a Million":

Immigrants and faggots
They make no sense to me.

The backlash was immediate. Radio refused to play the song. *Billboard* magazine excoriated the band. Certain promoters refused to market the record. Popular comedian Bobcat Goldthwait accused the band of writing the song just for the publicity. Vernon Reid, guitarist for Living Colour, a chart-topping African American *rock* band whose very existence (and success) challenged ideas around race in the music industry at the time, and fan of GNR, called Axl out publicly as well.

Axl claimed that the song was about a real-life experience he had at a bus station in Hollywood. It was reality and therefore, in his mind, worthy of documenting. However, the actual reality was that Axl was leveling a haymaker at the press, who he must have known would react intensely in response to his highly offensive lyrics. It was the sixteen-year-old in Lafayette lashing out but this time at a bigger strawman and under a much bigger spotlight.

But somehow, none of it mattered. The album was an immense seller.

Album sales weren't negatively affected, but the intensity of the public backlash was almost unbearable for Axl. He grew more manic. And then more depressed. He doubled down on therapy and through analysis uncovered "recovered memories" of sexual abuse as a child. He claimed publicly that he had been sexually assaulted by his real father who had, as Axl was now able to remember, raped him as a two-year-old. With psychotherapy, Axl felt himself making progress, but toward what he didn't exactly know. A torrent of pain, shame, and high-pitched anger raged inside of him stronger and more intensely than ever before, and he was about to blow.

Backstage at the Riverport Amphitheatre, in St. Louis, Missouri, in 1991, Guns N' Roses cooled their jets. You could tell just by looking at them that they were one of the biggest rock 'n' roll bands in the world. But the band Axl Rose had started back in Los Angeles six years earlier had begun to fade away. *This* band assembled before him, half-assedly working out its preshow jitters was a damaged, barely functioning version of its prefame self. Three years of hardcore drug and alcohol addiction and high-stress offstage drama had resulted in their current state.

Slash lived in constant fear of dying of AIDS. He believed there was a coming LA Metal AIDS epidemic and that if he or David Lee Roth caught it, then it was all over; the entire metal scene would be wiped out. His band members most definitely included. Slash was also desperately trying to kick heroin under threat from Axl to quit the band if he didn't. He was chipping occasionally, but for the most part he'd had it under control ever since Axl, *while opening for the Rolling Stones* onstage at the Los Angeles Memorial Coliseum, threatened to quit the band, saying to the audience, "Unless certain people in this band...get their shit together...these will be the last Guns N' Roses shows you will fucking ever see. 'Cause I'm tired of too many people, in this organization DANCING WITH MISTER GODDAMNED BROWNSTONE!"

Unlike Slash, Izzy got the message. It was a combination of Axl's threat and seeing his hero, Stones guitarist Keith Richards, up close and personal cheating death throughout middle age. What were the odds that a second Chuck Berry–obsessed guitarist in one of the world's greatest rock 'n' roll bands would also escape heroin's mortal grip and live to see his forties? Izzy didn't know the answer, but he knew his odds weren't good. So he gave up dancing with every kind of intoxicant, but as a result he now barely interacted with his bandmates and elected to travel via his own tour bus with his smokeshow of a girlfriend rather than fly with the traveling party, including groupies, on the band's chartered plane.

Steven Adler either refused or was simply unable to give up heroin, and he was unceremoniously kicked out of the band.

Duff, depressed from splitting with his wife, had retreated into his own bummed-out alcoholic nightmare while his new bandmates, drummer Matt Sorum and newly added keyboard player Dizzy Reed, did their best to fit into the highly dysfunctional band.

A band that was under immense pressure to deliver a follow-up album that would outperform their massively successful debut. The recording of said follow-up was wrought with tension. Axl's bandmates seldom appeared in the studio at the same time as he did, for fear of running up against his violent mood swings and thus sandbagging whatever slogging progress they'd made up to that point. The album was recorded piecemeal and at times by remote committee. The exact opposite of *Appetite for Destruction*, which was a short, frenetic shotgun blast of a musical statement made by five guys living the same life, dealing with the same problems and trying to get to the same place at the same time. That simplicity of intent was gone now. Axl was trying to make a grand creative statement while various members of his band were at times trying to work around dysfunctions: addiction, newfound fame, and an increasingly volatile and uncompromising lead singer.

Said lead singer sat backstage and watched his rhythm guitar player bang out the riff to Chuck Berry's "Sweet Little Sixteen" on his unplugged Telecaster. The strings eventually popped and snapped themselves into the chord progression for Elvis Presley's "Heartbreak Hotel"; the version that Izzy and Axl had used to steal the show out from under Tom Petty at MTV's Video Music Awards a few years back. Axl loved Elvis. He was the King. And Axl saw in himself some of that same ordained royalty. But Elvis was a nice boy and Axl was anything but... and he knew it. He crossed his arms and subconsciously ran his hand over the VICTORY OR DEATH tattoo on his left biceps. The yellow-and-red regimental emblem was the same design that Elvis wore on his hat in *G.I. Blues*. Maybe the outcome of the slogan wasn't so either/or, though. What if you could achieve both? Victory *and* death?

The pure rock 'n' roll days of the Ritz show were long gone. These days, Guns N' Roses were a worldwide phenom. The greatest rock 'n' roll band on the planet. Guns N' Roses were the real deal and very nearly coming apart at the seams because of it: victory *and* death.

Life at the moment for Axl and the rest of the band was *tense*, but backstage things were calm. While Izzy fingered his guitar, Slash—oblivious—fucked with the FM dial on a transistor radio and nursed a bottle of Jack Daniel's. Duff mixed up his hundredth vodka cranberry, his head somewhere else entirely. Matt warmed up with a drum pad; an endless triple-stroke drum roll, eighth-note triplets, then sixteenth-note triplets that were both only slightly out of time with Izzy's riff. Matt dropped the beat indiscriminately to sip cold domestic from a can. This being St. Louis, the domestic was

Clydesdale piss from the brewery of Messrs. Anheuser and Busch. Dizzy was nowhere in sight, off somewhere chasing skirt, taking advantage of his new fame. Axl was quiet, sipping champagne.

Preshow jitters time was the one time the band could stand each other's presence. They waited. Bonded by the incredibly rare reality they were about to go through together. Something very few people on the planet ever experience; the adoration of twenty thousand screaming fans who all want to either be you or fuck you. The exact type of rare experience that can bond you together and overcome even the deepest divisions.

Axl had "One in a Million" on his mind. It had been a while since they performed it. Who needed the headache? Axl took this as a defeat of sorts. Despite the controversy surrounding the song's lyrics, it was still a good song. Axl toyed with the idea of sneaking it into the set that night, but the thought was short-lived. It was nearly showtime, the only time of day that mattered.

GNR took the stage to a packed and rabid house. By now the band had their stage show wired tight. Axl insisted they fly by the seat of their spandex and Levis without a set list to keep it fresh, but the band did rely on a handful of sequential songs guaranteed to drive audiences wild. "Welcome to the Jungle" and then a downshift into the anthemic ballad, "Civil War." After that, a drum solo from Matt so Axl could suck on an oxygen mask backstage, then a guitar solo from Slash into the theme from *The Godfather* and finally into the barn-burning "Rocket Queen" to close the show.

The crowd recognized the song the instant the drums picked up. They knew this was the closer. Their last moments of the show to dig in and enjoy, to stay transported off in that place far away from the realities of the real world, from their shitty jobs, their parents, their schools. They pumped their fists, danced, sang along, and did their best to rage with their rock gods onstage in front of them.

From the blinding stage lights Axl could only see them swaying en masse. Flashback to Donington. He ripped into the first verse.

He wondered about security. Upfront it was lax. To Axl, the security staff seemed more interested in the band than in protecting the crowd. Flashback to the Philly Spectrum. Fucking Pigs.

His anger shot up through his chest and into his throat. His breath quickened. The words to the second half of the verse came out rushed and erratic.

Axl homed in on a civilian in the first couple rows. Was that a fan or a member of the press snapping photos? The press were only allowed a certain amount of sanctioned pictures per show, and the band was to be captured during set times at the *beginning* of their set and from the confines of the camera well up in front of the stage only, *not from within the audience*. Oftentimes a performer will remove a piece of clothing after the allotted period of time, so that if a media outlet runs a photo of the performer *without* that scarf on, or *without* that leather jacket, then everybody knows that media outlet broke the rules. Axl boiled. Fucking press. Give them an inch and they take a goddamn mile. The press did whatever the hell they liked. Wrote whatever the hell they wanted. Spread whatever fucking rumors they felt like spreading. They had carte blanche to fuck with you just like the pigs in Philly. Just like the West Holly-wood sheriff's deputies and most definitely just like the hick cops back in Lafayette. They were *all* out to get him. To take advantage of him. Just like his father had done.

As he sang out the chorus, Axl focused on the dude in the audience taking pictures. Shit. It was worse than he thought. Dude wasn't taking photos, he was videotaping! Axl got three lines deep before it all became too much to take. He stopped singing and screamed into the mic,

"HEY! Take that! Take that. NOW. Get that guy and take that!"
Axl had stopped singing completely and was pointing at the dude

with the camera imploring security to stop him. Axl could see now. Dude wasn't a member of the press. He was a biker. Nobody did anything. Axl raged at the inaction. Here he was. Helpless again. The band, confused, continued the chorus behind him.

Fuck this, Axl thought. Press member, biker, whatever. It didn't matter. When not one member of the venue's security team moved to help him, Axl literally flew into action. He barked into the mic, "I'LL TAKE IT, GODDAMMIT" before slamming the mic down and diving headfirst into the audience to solve the problem himself. The band, almost on cue, resolved the chorus and began muddling through an instrumental version of the second verse while their singer went at it—wildly throwing punches in the first few rows. Axl, unaware of who he was fucking with, began manically flailing and seriously pissing off members of the Saddle Tramps motor-cycle club. Local security knew where their bread was buttered and went at Axl instead of at the bikers. Axl resisted. Kicking, punching at everyone in sight. When it became clear that security wasn't helping, GNR's roadies entered the fray and pulled Axl back up onstage, but not before he landed a full-fisted punch in the grill of one of the crowd members who'd got up in his face.

Once he was back on stage Axl grabbed the mic, pissed, and quickening his pace toward the side of the stage, "Well! Thanks to the lame-ass security, I'm going home." And with that he slammed the mic into the stage and stormed off. Slash leaned into a mic and added a casual, "We're outta here."

That was it. Show over.

The crowd was stunned. Confused. No one moved. No one knew what was going on. GNR's roadies quickly went about breaking down the band's gear. A clear signal that the show was definitely done. The party was over. Guns N' Roses weren't coming back. Beer cans began raining down on the stage from the audience. The boos started. At first a smattering and then the chorus of an angry mob. The roadies were pissed and rightly so. They began to taunt the audience, inciting them even more.

Drunk, angry, and violent, the audience turned on itself. The Saddle Tramps went alpha, erupting on anyone who got in their way while making their exit. A naked man ran around the floor frantically, blood pouring from a wound in his head. The police descended to restore order and were openly challenged by fans. Beatings commenced. Batons. Steel-toed kicks to the skull. A chant of "Fuck You, Pigs" rose up from the audience.

The crowd started ripping up the chairs from the floor. Pulling them apart and launching them to the stage. The cops reeled out the fire hose and attempted to use it to beat back the crowd, but the water pressure was so weak the audience began moving *toward* the water to cool off and thus toward the stage. One of the giant video screens on the side of the stage was pulled down. The massive sixty-ton sound and light rig lurched uncomfortably from side to side as idiotic fans swung from its cables. Riverport was about to make Donington look like a walk in the park until the cops broke out a tear gas–like substance and got hold of the situation.

In the end it was a bloody riot that Axl Rose's deep well of anger had incited: sixty-five people badly injured, twenty-five of them police officers. Dozens arrested, and hundreds of thousands of dollars in property damage. Axl was eventually charged with four counts of assault and one for property damage. The jury found him guilty and the judge fined him $50,000. It was worth it, Axl thought. They all had it coming.

After he stormed offstage, the band's road crew swept into action, endeavoring to get the band away without further incident or arrest. They exited out the back under a deluge of flying glass bottles from angry fans who had by now made their way around to the backside of the venue. The tour bus was too easy a mark. And the limos were out of the question, so all six band members dove into a nondescript passenger van and hid on the floor, out of sight from the gathering mob as they made their escape.

They were traveling together again. Just like the old days back in LA. Before the fame. Before the chaos and the pressure of success. Axl was too keyed up to reflect on the irony: that his anger and mood swings that had contributed so significantly to driving the band apart as of late, were the exact things bringing them together at this very moment en route from one gig to the next. Hoping, just as they had in the beginning, to escape arrest in time to get to the stage for the next show. With a roadie behind the wheel and the band members outstretched on the floor, the van raced through the streets of St. Louis.

It was a good half an hour before they raised themselves up off the van's floor to look out of their windows, and it was lucky they did. Izzy watched as they passed a sign for Wentzville. Wentzville was where his hero, Chuck Berry, lived. Izzy knew enough rock 'n' roll history to realize that Wentzville was *west* of St. Louis, Missouri. *West.* The dumbass roadie behind the wheel had them heading the opposite way they were supposed to be going. They needed to be driving toward Illinois and their next gig in Chicago, home of the blues and home to another one of Izzy's heroes, the signifying Bo Diddley, and also home of Chess Records, where Chuck Berry made his greatest records.

CHAPTER 6

CHUCK BERRY

CHUCK BERRY COULDN'T SLEEP. Not on his government-issued mattress anyway. Not in the fifteen-by-fifteen-foot cell with the two other prisoners he was forced to shack up with. And not without sex. *Horny* wasn't strong enough a word. Chuck Berry was driven to distraction. Who thought it wise to staff this place with *female* security officers? There weren't a lot, but hell, one female was one too many. And these women were easy on the eyes. Long hair. Heels. Curves for days. Chuck knew he was in trouble. So he wrote.

Chuck Berry loved words. The way they showed up for him and then rolled off his tongue and out onto the page. First as poetry. Then, later in life, as songs. And behind bars he wrote both. The aptly titled "No Particular Place to Go," "Nadine (Is It You?)" "Carol," and "You Never Can Tell" were among the songs Chuck had written during his second stretch in lockup, back in 1962. This current stint was different. He was older. Wiser. And had more mileage in the rearview. It was 1979 and Chuck Berry was hell-bent on using his time away to write his autobiography and to set the record straight. But the women changed everything. Chuck couldn't focus. Keeping his thoughts off sex, the kind of sex that lands you in jail—or keeps you in jail—*that* was a problem. There was only so much of the mess-around he could do by himself, so he wrote what his fellow inmates called "Chuck's Good Stories." They were pure sex. Bluer than a Redd Foxx party record. Chuck Berry, America's greatest cultural export since jazz, in an effort to keep himself from spinning off the planet from a lack of sex in the pen, penned down-and-dirty fuck fiction.

As far as prison was concerned, Charles Edward Anderson Berry, aka Chuck Berry, aka "the man who invented rock 'n' roll," wasn't really bothered by it. It was the reason he was locked up that bothered him immensely. Sentenced to 120 days for tax evasion in 1979 was bunk. He was guilty, sure. One hundred and twenty grand or so unreported to Uncle Sam is legit tax evasion, but come on. Despite previously serving two prison sentences—one a ten-year stint, of which he served three, for armed robbery at the age of seventeen and one for violating the Mann Act, a beef that sent him to the federal pen for a year and a half in 1962 to serve legit, hard time— Chuck couldn't help but think that had he not been "Chuck Berry," the rock 'n' roller, he would have been given the opportunity to work out a deal with authorities for the relatively harmless white-collar crime he had committed. Chuck knew that the real reason he was in jail was because he was a black man who enjoyed his freedom just a *little* too freely in a white man's world. But being alone? Nah, it wasn't all that bad.

Chuck was used to it. In fact, he preferred it. From an early age, he learned to occupy that big brain of his. First with the family radio. Sitting alone, as a twelve-year-old, in his living room at 4319 Labadie Street in St. Louis, Missouri, listening to various jazz, blues, big band, and boogie-woogie artists popular at the time: Ella Fitzgerald, Big Joe Turner, Benny Goodman, Jelly Roll Morton, and Fats Waller were among his favorites. Then with his camera. His friend Harry had a darkroom, and Chuck loved it. The solitude, the attention to detail, the way it slowed down the world around him, and of course, the way it sped up his heart rate whenever pinup photos circulated through in need of development. Women, some of them white, in nearly see-through lingerie flirting with him from beyond the lens. Out of the darkroom they were strictly off-limits, but here, among the smell of the Eastman Kodak chemicals and within the climate-controlled temperature, he could at least speak to them if nothing else.

Chuck dug the singular nature of it all. It gave him time to think about the things that teenage boys think about. To think about where he was. Who he was and what he wanted out of his life. And it gave him time to think about poetry. He put poems together in his head to pass the time. And soon he would begin to think about that poetry as music.

Being alone was where it was at. It was how Chuck liked it. Even years later, while he was at the height of his success and financially able to employ bands big enough to rival his beloved Count Basie's orchestra, Chuck preferred—no, *insisted*—on traveling alone. With no band. Just him, his guitar, and an open road. He didn't even carry a guitar cord, never mind an amplifier. He'd roll from town to town in one of his late-model coffee-colored Cadillacs stone alone. No manager. No roadie. No handlers and no accompanying musicians. At about thirty minutes before showtime, he'd pull up to whatever ten- to twenty-thousand-capacity venue he was head-lining that night near the backstage entrance, park wherever the hell he wanted, waltz into the promoter's office confidently, and politely demand payment in advance. In cash. And usually—under the threat of not performing—extort an extra $1,000 cherry on top before going onstage.

Once satisfied that the pockets of his polyester bell bottoms were properly lined, he'd walk on stage with his Gibson ES-335. Straight past his backing band—a combo of local musicians he'd yet to meet who stood scared shitless, with their instruments readied for the Great Chuck Berry's cue. Chuck would then plug his guitar into whatever amp the promoter had set up for him and proceed to tune his guitar—loudly—in front of the entire auditorium and then, without having said one word or making any eye contact at all with his new band, he'd launch into one of his classic opening riffs and drag the terrified musicians along with him for a clumsy but exhilarating ride.

Even onstage, playing with other people in front of thousands of fans, he was alone. In his own head while playing the hits and mugging for the crowd, occasionally allowing himself to get lost in tearing the ass out of one of his guitar solos. If he was really feeling it, by midset he'd turn to his band and playfully shout, "Play for that money, boys!" and if they were lucky (and good) he'd kick a grand back to them after the show on top of whatever the promoter was paying. But more often than not, he was gone after the last encore, without a word. Usually before the house lights were even on. Sometimes before the band had even finished the outro to his last song. Drifting off down some American highway into the night. Words moving through his head in slow motion. His guitar in its case, strapped in vertically in the passenger seat to his right, but otherwise he was totally alone.

And so what? Chuck Berry didn't need a band. He was Chuck Berry. Bands were just another expense. Another hassle. And who needed more hassle? Life was filled with them, going back as far as he could remember. Especially in St. Louis, Missouri in the 1930s and '40s. It wasn't quite the Deep South, but it was a racist social construct filled with hassles from as early as Chuck could remember. White cops were suspicious of everything you did, everywhere you went. Chuck learned to live with it. He had to. There was no other choice. But it wasn't easy, especially as he hit puberty. A young man's hormones don't see in black and white, and Chuck burned for what Sam Cooke would later refer to as "the snow"—that is, sleeping with white women. But any sort of interracial romantic relationship was strictly taboo and likely to land a young black man in jail or, worse, swinging from a rope at the end of a poplar tree. In St. Louis at the time, if a black man and a white woman were stopped by a cop, they were at the very least immediately hauled into the police station for mandatory venereal disease shots.

A young Chuck tried not to stare at the bat. If he fixated on it, they'd be more likely to use it. Under the high-watt fluorescent lightbulb in the St. Louis district police headquarters' interrogation room, he tried not to look at anything at all. But his eyes just couldn't help glancing back to the bat.

The 1949 Louisville Slugger was an especially strong baseball bat, but in the years following World War II, after having served its country by supplying the U.S. Army with wooden gunstocks and billy clubs, the Louisville Slugger company took its wartime knowledge and improved upon what was previously considered perfect, the Model 125. Turning it out of select second growth ash wood, Louisville Slugger created a new batch of incredibly powerful bats. The stick of choice for all-timers like Joe DiMaggio and Ted Williams. Oil tempered and finished in a distinct saddle tan finish, the 1949 Model 125—being born from war—was imbued with violence.

Chuck Berry knew none of this as he sweated and kept looking to and fro, trying to find some appropriate place for his eyes to land as he tried not to stare at the men across the table from him in a confrontational way, or at that damn baseball bat. All he could think of were his brains being painted onto the wall if the police sergeant positioned above him with the Model 125 Louisville Slugger cocked on his shoulder decided to get all Stan Musial and swing at Chuck's skull for the cheap seats. Two on. Nobody out.

"Did ya fugger?" asked the police captain. Sergeant Stan The Man kept the bat held high, staring right through Chuck, sitting hot in the box. Daring him to say the wrong thing.

Chuck lobbed one straight down the middle, "No sir. A white woman? No sir!"

Chuck was scared. He'd been informed, after being picked up by the cops on a tip by a jilted boyfriend of a white girl he'd been messing around with, that if one word of his statement was a lie, Sergeant Stan The Man would swing for the fences.

Even then Chuck knew what his audience wanted; they wanted fear. The racist white cops needed to feel like they were in control. So Chuck gave them what they wanted. He was indeed legitimately frightened, but now he played to the cheap seats, laying it on thick. Overdramatizing a wince here and a shudder there until finally, both the captain and the sergeant broke into laughter. Amused at what they believed they had done: brought a young black man to his knees. He was eventually let go, but the gravity of the incident was never lost on him. He knew the cops could have killed him at their will and no doubt frame it up as justifiable. From then on, Chuck would think twice about which women he slept with and where.

But regardless, thinking about sleeping with women was most of what he did in prison. And there was lots to think about. Chuck Berry had been a successful entertainer for most of his adult life. Women were never a problem. Or, depending on how Chuck looked at it, women were *always* a problem.

Chuck Berry: Stone alone en route to the next gig.

Even before he was "Chuck Berry," he was Chuck Berry, which is to say he was a tall, charismatic, brown-eyed handsome man. And he invented rock 'n' roll.

It started at the Crank Club on Venderventer in St. Louis, Missouri, back in 1954 with the Chuck Berry Combo: Chuck on guitar and vocals, drummer Ebby Hardy, and piano player Johnnie Johnson. The sets were long and the audiences were a demanding mix of black and white country and blues fans. For musicians at the time, if you wanted to keep the gig, you needed to keep the patrons dancing. Make them thirsty enough to keep buying drinks. Chuck caught on quick. When it came to music, Missouri was largely hillbilly country. So Chuck laid it down for the white audience. He overemphasized his diction like the country artists he'd heard on the radio and projected his voice hard over that fast country backbeat. When it came time for a break, Chuck leaned on his hero Nat King Cole's repertoire. St. Louis wasn't entirely unsophisticated, and Nat's songs were well known to both black and white music fans. Chuck's voice and personality were naturally suited to deliver Nat's velvety melodies. And to bring it on home again, Chuck dug down into the Delta for those Muddy Waters songs that got him at his core. The band's regular weekend performances had a predictable rhythm to them. The audience loved it and continuously came back for more.

His band took it all in stride. Understanding that it was the Chuck show. That it was his name in lights. They backed him with the requisite balance of group support and individual personality, but long sets coupled with even the most diverse repertoire of traditional blues, country, and jazz can get stale for the musicians playing it over and over again. The Chuck Berry Combo began to experiment.

Chuck and Johnnie developed a natural call-and-response on guitar and piano. The crowd ate it up. Particularly on the fast numbers. Chuck grew bored with the songs from other artists that he was covering and began putting his own words to the familiar country and blues chord progressions. Within no time, Chuck was writing his own tunes. His poetry now had a beat.

The combo stretched out in these originals in front of the crowd at the Crank Club. Johnnie would eventually tire of playing the rhythm on piano (keeping that left hand pulsing along all night was real work). He'd give it a rest and let his right hand drift lazily along the high keys in response to whatever Chuck was spitting out for vocals. In effect, they created a vacuum. A rhythm vacuum. And without a bass player in the combo, there was a void where there was once a piano pounding out the rhythm in tandem with the drums. The audience picked up on the letdown. Their disinterest was palpable to Chuck. Rather than lay it all back on Johnnie, Chuck figured out how to play Johnnie's piano rhythm by himself, on guitar. He heavily emphasized the second and fourth beats instead of accenting every downbeat. In doing so, Chuck had molded the traditional country/rhythm and blues piano rhythm into what has become the single most influential element in all of rock 'n' roll: Chuck Berry's *rhythm* guitar riff.

Chuck's *rhythm* guitar riff, not to be confused with his two-string *lead* riff, "the Chuck Berry lick" that introduces many of his greatest hits and is the guitar part he is most identified with. Chuck's rhythm riff is the thread that ties together the most influential rock 'n' roll artists of all time, and this riff did not fully exist before Chuck Berry. Guitar players know it well. It's the root 6 or root 5 power chord that stretches the pinky up two frets on the neck. Non–guitar players, think of the rhythm guitar part appropriated by Marty McFly in *Back to the Future*.

This is the same riff that the most consequential guitar players of all time could not leave alone. The Beatles and the Rolling Stones recorded it in their covers of early Berry classics and then morphed it into something of their own with "Back in the U.S.S.R." and "Get Back" from the Beatles, and "Midnight Rambler" and "Rip This Joint" from the Stones.

Jimmy Page, Eric Clapton, Jeff Beck, and Pete Townshend borrowed it. The Beach Boys rewrote Chuck's "Sweet Little Sixteen," turning it into "Surfin' USA." Jimi Hendrix, ZZ Top's Billy Gibbons, and Stevie Ray Vaughan all hung their wide-brimmed hats on the riff. AC/DC built their careers on the back of the riff, and seminal punk rock bands like the New York Dolls, the Ramones, the Sex Pistols, and the Clash sped the riff up and nearly drove it off the road. Guns N' Roses, Green Day, and more recently the White Stripes, the Black Keys, and Low Cut Connie have all incorporated it into their songwriting.

Sure, there are other towering and influential early rock 'n' roll figures, like Ike Turner, Buddy Holly, Little Richard, and even Elvis Presley, who contributed greatly to the form in its nascent years, but none of them have one singular contribution that is shared so widely among rock 'n' roll artists throughout each period of rock's history. Music journalists will tie themselves in knots trying to get you to bite down on the idea that the hard-strumming Sister Rosetta Tharpe invented rock 'n' roll, but her influence simply isn't palpable enough. Critics would also like you to believe that Ike Turner invented rock 'n' roll with Jackie Brenston's "Rocket 88" from 1951, a song that Ike wrote well before Chuck Berry began recording. They're right to point to the greatness of "Rocket 88," but the song is a *shuffle*, and rock 'n' roll grew its wings on the back of the straight-ahead backbeat. The shuffle was a signifier of the past. Rock 'n' roll was about the future. You can't give credit to Elvis Presley's "That's All Right" from 1954 because it's too hillbilly sounding, and Presley's "Heartbreak Hotel" from 1956 was genre defying but, as such, not genre *defining*. Little Richard? Jerry Lee Lewis? Not enough guitar. Rock 'n' roll grew into a guitar-dominated genre of music, not a piano-dominated genre.

The term *rock 'n' roll* had been in use for a good while by the time Chuck came along, but it didn't come to be defined as a genre or fully realized stylistically until Chuck Berry recorded and released "Rock and Roll Music" in 1957. This song is rock 'n' roll's big bang. It is the first rock 'n' roll song, and it has nothing to do with the song's title. It's about everything else: the beat, the lyrics and the production—but it's especially about Chuck's rhythm guitar. It's the first recorded appearance of his signature riff on the airwaves. The riff that he took out of his piano player's hands and then shredded through his tiny, distorted amp.

Chuck Berry's innovation and artful melding of country and rhythm and blues would soon launch him out of the Crank Club and into a chance meeting with his hero, Muddy Waters, which would in turn lead him to a recording contract with Chess Records. His first single for Chess, "Maybellene," was quick to blanket the airwaves, and Chuck Berry was on his way.

"Maybellene" hit No. 1 on the R&B charts and No. 5 on the pop chart. And it was largely due to the efforts of a DJ in New York named Alan Freed. Freed spun the song one night on his show for two hours straight. One song. Over and over again. For two hours straight. When Chuck heard, he was shocked at the passion Freed had shown for his song, but that would wear off quickly when Chuck learned that the DJ was credited alongside Chuck as one of the songwriters of "Maybellene" in a scam set up by Leonard Chess (owner of Chess Records), who gave Freed songwriting credit as an incentive to spin the song and rack up publishing royalties to line his pockets with. Chuck Berry had just learned the most important lesson in the music business the hard way: Never trust your record label.

Regardless, the song was a hit and Chuck was a star and touring frequently. All over America. From the Midwest to New England to the Deep South. It being the 1950s, traveling through the Deep South as a successful young black man was not easy and was downright dangerous if you weren't careful.

Chuck didn't mean to kiss her. She threw herself at him. Right there onstage. In front of everyone. Chuck was feeling loose. His set was tight. The crowd was jazzed. The adrenaline from everyone on- and offstage was pumping. It was a small, intimate dance for some college students in a renovated Army barracks in Meridian, Mississippi. The girl couldn't have been younger than eighteen. It didn't matter. Her tongue, when it hit his, took him completely out of the moment and delivered him to someplace far away. His mouth sunk into hers. Right there on the stage. Under the house lights that were now on and blasting down upon the couple. The moment didn't last. Chuck snapped himself out of it and pulled away. This was Mississippi. She was white. He was black.

When he opened his eyes, she was staring at him as if to say, *What's the matter? Don't you want me?* A question he would have happily answered if it weren't for the staring eyes of the rest of the crowd, which now—a few minutes removed from his performance—had snapped back to reality. The crowd had just witnessed a black man kissing a white girl in a segregated hall where the black kids weren't even allowed to sit next to white kids. That was Chuck's cue. He unplugged his guitar, quietly stepped off the stage, and made his way to the side door of the makeshift auditorium under the glaring eyes of the crowd.

The place was stone-cold quiet. Chuck was nearly at the door. Nearly free until a frat boy rose up in front of Chuck flanked by seven of his brothers. Big. White. Dumb.

"Chuck, did you try to date my sister?"

Chuck was quick to the point, "No, of course not!"

Another lunkhead, this one to the side of the original frat boy pointed at Chuck and shouted, "He did! He's a Yankee like the rest of 'em!"

This was the cue for the other frat boys to chime in with their own racist accusations. The crowd turned on Chuck. Boos were swelling up from throughout the auditorium. Chuck could feel the fear. It cooled the sweat on his skin.

That's when he saw it. The gleam of the switchblade. Extended menacingly from the hand of the first lunkhead. The promoter saw it, too. Fearing the worst, he decided to play peacemaker and jumped between the knife and Chuck, pushing him aside. Chuck, while being dragged away, out of the mob and backward toward the exit, started singing. It was an unconscious, visceral attempt to quash the violence in the air: "It was a teenage wedding and the old folks wished them well."

The boos continued. So did the shouting.

Chuck shouted/sang back, "You could see that Pierre did truly love the mademoiselle."

Lunkhead wasn't having it. Enraged and now being held back by a small basketball squad, and still holding his switchblade, he was quick to get lippy: "I'm a Mississippian…and this nigger asked my sister for a date!" Lunkhead grew more upset and struggled to break away from his classmates to tear Chuck limb from limb.

Chuck shouted/sang more lyrics at him: "And now the young monsieur and madame have rung the chapel bell."

Chuck was pushed out of harm's way and out the exit door into the night, where he was soon greeted by Mississippi's finest and hauled in. For what exactly, he wasn't told. He was kept in jail overnight but he was alive. In the morning he was driven to the airport, but only after being relieved of the $700 he'd made from the previous night's show by the cops. *C'est la vie*, thought Chuck.

Chuck experienced plenty of racism back home in St. Louis as well despite his growing fame, and not just from lunkhead frat boys. Judges, particularly the judge presiding over his appeal for the charge that he violated the Mann Act. Chuck was hauled in before a gig at Club Bandstand, his club in St. Louis, on December 23, 1959. Violating the Mann Act was a serious charge. Designed to cut down on human trafficking and prevent the transport and thus spreading of prostitution, it was nefariously used by authorities to target high-profile black men (see boxer Jack Johnson as exhibit A to Chuck Berry as exhibit B).

Chuck was fucked. The cops said she was only fourteen. And white*ish*. Chuck thought she was American Indian. The authorities didn't care. She was underage and thus she was the hammer they were going to use to bust up Chuck Berry and his nightclub. The one that cops viewed as a black mark on the image of white purity that the city wanted to project. Club Bandstand was where the girl worked after Chuck brought her up in his Cadillac from El Paso across state lines, thus committing—according to the Mann Act— "white slavery." Her age wasn't the only problem. St. Louis cops got wind of her because they'd heard about the young, exotic-looking girl working over at Chuck's place who was tricking herself out.

Chuck stood trial and faced ten years in prison. Hard time. After two weeks, the all-white-male jury found him guilty. The racist judge gave him five years. Chuck appealed, successfully claiming and proving bias on behalf of the judge and had his sentence dropped down to three years. He eventually had the sentence reduced to a year and a half, but in the end the cops got what they wanted. In Chuck's absence, Club Bandstand went under and closed. Chuck served his time but he was never the same afterward. He was no angel, but he wasn't what authorities claimed he was, either. He was a target. He was a marked man. It was unjust, and Chuck was unable to accept it.

Chuck Berry seldom thought about these incidents. They were just his life. Other people had their problems. Chuck had his. So what? Best to just keep your head down and keep your mind occupied. Especially in prison. Chuck's writing was enough to keep him busy. He had just finished the sixteenth chapter in his autobiography, one that detailed his midcareer rise to the top of the pop charts in 1972 with the release of the novelty song, "My Ding-a-Ling." The tune was a schoolyard version of the erotica he would later come to write from his cell. Filled with sly innuendo and a singsongy chorus, it was a joke. Chuck was as surprised as anyone at its success. But the money poured in.

Chuck took part of his earnings and used it to indulge his new hobby: videography, an extension of the interest in photography that he'd had since childhood. Chuck purchased the video company Corplex, and rolled it and its assets (including the company's employees) into a new company he'd incorporated called Chuck Berry Communication Systems, Inc. At the time of Chuck's writing he estimated he had spent more than three quarters of a million dollars in electronic equipment to indulge his fascination with photography and videography, specifically the three-quarter-inch video-mixing editor set he had back at his home in Berry Park.

Berry Park was Chuck's dream brought to life. For a minute anyway. Chuck, smartly, began investing in real estate as soon as he started making real money. Berry Park was his answer to the exclusive, all-white country clubs that he and his father would

Two-three count, nobody on, he hit a high fly into the stands. He also invented rock 'n' roll.

service as carpenters and handymen back when he was a boy. Clubs that would pay him a meager wage but never allow him to join. Berry Park sat on thirty acres about forty miles outside St. Louis in Wentzville, Missouri. When it opened in August 1960, it was a sparkling and integrated utopic realization of mid-century America. Guests swam in the guitar-shaped swimming pool, hunted in the woods, fished in the pond, and danced in the lodge. The park succeeded in its early years, for about as long as Chuck could keep his eyes on it, but by the close of the decade, with Chuck's constant touring and legal troubles, the property eventually fell into a seedy, bleak existence. The country club was shuttered. As a business, Berry Park pivoted to a residential real estate venture owned by Chuck, where he would rent rooms and trailers on the property to locals while he continued to reside in the "big house" on the property.

After Chuck's stretch for tax evasion, he went back to Berry Park, continued to perform and to diversify financially, investing in local real estate and restaurants. By all accounts Chuck's tenants and employees were happy. All but one: Hosana A. Huck.

Mrs. Huck, a cook at Wentzville's Southern Air Restaurant, was a very disgruntled employee. In 1989 the *St. Louis Post-Dispatch* reported that Huck had filed a civil suit for invasion of privacy against the owner of the Southern Air Restaurant; Charles Edward Anderson Berry, aka Chuck Berry.

The headline read: CHUCK BERRY TAPED WOMEN, SUIT CHARGES.

The article stated that "a suit accuses rock 'n' roll pioneer Chuck Berry of videotaping women as they used the women's room at his Southern Air Restaurant in Wentzville... The suit alleges that the videotapes 'were created for the improper purpose of the entertainment and gratification' of what it describes as Berry's 'sexual fetishes and sexual predilections.'"

Chuck Berry didn't judge. Who was he to say what was right and what was wrong between two consenting adults? *Consenting* being the key word. Chuck's employee, Mrs. Huck, alleged that she did not consent to being videotaped. She alleged that her employer, the musician with the keen interest in videography and former owner of a video company, secretly videotaped her urinating to get himself off.

Unfortunately for Chuck Berry, there were tapes. Lots and lots of tapes. How they surfaced and came into the hands of authorities is a matter of debate. Mrs. Huck, who filed the initial claim against Chuck, made her statement to authorities after her husband, a handyman who also worked for Chuck, supposedly *found* a box of videotapes in a trash dumpster on public Wentzville property (not on Chuck Berry's property), and when he stumbled upon this cardboard box of lewd and scandalous VHS tapes—*that happened to contain videos of his own wife*—there just *happened* to be two of St. Louis's finest on hand to witness Mr. Huck's discovery.

It could not be claimed that Mr. Huck took possession of the tapes illegally. How could it? He found them. In a public place. And there were cops there who could back him up.

The tapes told their own story. And it was not a good one. There were numerous recordings, all with big-bosomed blondes. Chuck denied they were his, along with two other tapes with hundreds of women; all white, relieving themselves. They were filmed surreptitiously from cameras positioned behind toilet seats. Close-ups. From the front and the back. Footage was expertly spliced together with a second camera positioned above the toilet to capture the wide shots of the women before and after relieving themselves. And these clips were all edited together into compilation reels with various shots being frozen in time for lasting effect. The women, for the most part, were adults. But there was also footage of girls under the age of ten.

After the tapes were found, Berry Park was raided. Small amounts of marijuana, what looked like hash, $122,501 in cash, and fifty-nine more VHS tapes were hauled out of Chuck's home.

County Prosecutor William J. Hannah took too big a swing and tried to claim that not only was Chuck Berry a sexual predator but also a major drug player, dealing millions of dollars in cocaine.

Nothing had changed from the '50s. St. Louis authorities were still out to break Chuck Berry. Even when they seemed to have him dead to rights on legitimate charges, they couldn't resist swinging for the fences instead of taking the bloop single to safely advance their case.

Public opinion turned on them, and a *St. Louis Post-Dispatch* editorial claimed the prosecutor was "showboating" and plainly looking to advance his own career. Nevertheless, Chuck was charged with marijuana possession and child abuse. Missouri law stated that featuring young people, naked, on video constitutes child abuse.

Chuck turned himself in.

He sued for the return of his tapes.

He sued the lawyers.

He sued the plaintiffs.

The women spoke up. They'd had it with the man known around Berry Park as "Charles."

Sharissa Kistner, who lived on Chuck's property with her mom in one of the trailers, claimed that Chuck approached her one day and told her that he could see her in her room from his mansion. According to Sharissa, he said that he was "thinking of you yesterday while I was playing with myself."

Chuck wasn't deterred. He sued the grandstanding prosecutor, who subsequently lost his reelection bid. With that, the prosecutor's office dropped the child abuse charges. In turn, Chuck dropped his suit against the prosecutor and pleaded guilty only to the marijuana charge. He got what amounted to a slap on the wrist: two years probation for the weed and an agreement to pay $5,000 to a local substance abuse program.

That took care of the authorities, but it didn't take care of the women.

They rolled their multiple beefs concerning Chuck's toilet tapes into one class action suit. Chuck paid out a reported $1.2 million in settlement fees to make the case go away.

Afterward, and for the rest of his life, Chuck was defiant in the face of his critics. What did they know about it? Videography to Chuck was merely self-expression. Just like music and poetry and sex. Rock 'n' roll had once been his outlet. In the early days anyway. When he was young and making young people's music, but for the majority of his life, rock 'n' roll—the music he invented—was just a job. "Chuck Berry" was the position he made for himself and filled. "Charles" was who he really was.

Chuck Berry was defiant but he wasn't angry. Later in life, his critics, the ones from the big newspapers and magazines back east, would from time to time attempt to get Chuck to cop to that rock 'n' roll racial resentment rap: The white man stealing from the black man, how did Chuck feel about being appropriated? That sort of thing. Chuck never took the bait, even if he knew he had a case. The critics' take was lazy and simple. They didn't get it. Chuck knew what his contribution was. He didn't need the "King of Rock 'n' Roll" moniker that Elvis had. Sure, he wouldn't mind Elvis's bank account or the freedom Elvis was allowed, to come and go as he pleased, to sleep with whomever he wanted, to be whoever he wanted to be, but Chuck was content with what he'd accomplished.

He admitted as much to the *New York Times* once: "Had I been pushed like Colonel Parker pushed Elvis, had I been a white boy like Elvis, sure, it would have been different." He regretted the comment as soon as it left his lips. Why let them see you sweat?

Why give them the satisfaction? Besides, what really bothered him was how racist attitudes affected who and how you could love. Free love was always a joke. Ask Sammy Davis Jr. about "free love." Chuck was unable to *love* how he wanted. And unlike the white artists who were starting out at the same time as him, Chuck couldn't express this injustice through music.

Rock 'n' roll was just that—rock 'n' roll. It stayed the same. No matter how much it changed. No matter who was playing it or what they were wearing. No matter what year it was. There was only one constant: Chuck Berry. One thread: his riff.

And Chuck had other interests he could rely on, explore, tinker with, and dabble in. Chuck was writing again and thinking about music. He wasn't writing about sex and he wasn't writing poems. He was giving his hand a spin at music criticism. And why not? What did the critics actually know, anyway? Nothing, that's what. He was Chuck Berry and he invented rock 'n' roll, so who better an authority to opine on this new type of music that the kids were all telling him was going to make rock 'n' roll obsolete—punk rock. Chuck was approached by some local kids who had a handmade 'zine called *Jet Lag* and asked to give his take on some of the more popular punk records that had come out over the past couple of years. Chuck thought that writing some record reviews would be fun. And it was. But as he expected, it was all just rock 'n' roll.

Chuck said of the Ramones' "Sheena Is a Punk Rocker": "A good little jump number. These guys remind me of myself when I first started. I only knew three chords too." And on "God Save the Queen" by the Sex Pistols, Chuck stated, "Can't understand most of the vocals. If you're going to be mad at least let the people know what you're mad about."

Chuck Berry wasn't mad. He was Chuck Berry. Charles Anderson Edward Berry? Now that guy had a legitimate beef. He also had some videotapes to edit and a second book to write.

Chuck Berry said so in the pages of his autobiography penned from behind bars: "Now that I know much more about the writing of a book, strangely enough I intend to go for another. One that I will enjoy, the true story of my sex life. It shall not infringe on anyone or thing but me and my excessive desire to continue melting the ice of American hypocrisy regarding behavior and beliefs that are now 'in the closet' and only surface in court, crime, or comical conversation."

God save Chuck Berry.

CHAPTER 7

SID VICIOUS

SID VICIOUS STARED DOWN into his lap. He thought for a half-second about that pervy Chuck Berry song, "My Ding-A-Ling," that had been an unexpected second-coming hit in England for Chuck when Sid was a teen. What a dumb song.

"I want to play with my ding-a-ling."

Sid laughed in spite of his predicament. He was always able to find *something* to laugh at, even now. But then reality always hit him and snapped him back hard.

It was the sign. The sign said, YOU ARE NOW ENTERING RIKERS ISLAND NEW YORK CITY PRISON COMPLEX, but it might as well have said, YOU ARE GOING TO DIE FROM DOPE SICKNESS. Because that was what was going through Sid Vicious's mind as he was bused into the infamous prison.

Sentenced for violating his parole after eight foggy weeks of freedom, a court trial was hanging over his head. From all accounts *Sid* wasn't even sure if he was guilty or not. The charge: murdering the love of his life, Nancy Spungen.

As a new prisoner to Rikers, Sid was stored in a cramped holding cell with the other new arrivals. It made no difference whether he was black or white or a gangster or a suit. Whether he was a dope fiend or mentally ill. There was no special treatment. Not even for a rock star. The holding cell was stuffed with inmates and there was zero privacy.

There were two long benches but not long enough for all of the inmates to sit. The other option was the disgusting floor. A sticky mix of dirt, blood, spit, piss, cigarette ash, and feces. The smell was overwhelming. It was all of that mixed with the odor of a thousand third world nation bazaars.

If Sid was lucky, the screws would have him sorted out in a couple hours and out of that shithole and off to fresh horrors like the open dorm he'd be living in until making bail or going to trial. This was a different kind of hell.

The open dorm holding cell was where Sid would work out his dope sickness: in the open, sweating it out next to sixty-four other inmates. No partitions, just a cot without barriers to fend off the hustlers and rapists. Prison is no place for the pretty and despite the thousand-yard junkie stare, the acne, and the butch haircut, Sid Vicious, with his high cheekbones and lanky demeanor, was indeed pretty. And famous. A tough burden to carry in Rikers, where rape was as certain as the shitty food.

But being raped wasn't the worst of Sid's problems. No access to heroin was higher on the "oh shit" list.

It was the end of 1978. An awful year if ever there was one for Sid Vicious. It began with so much promise: The Sex Pistols—the band he had only joined the year before—were on their first tour of the States. But that American foray, which began in January of '78, lasted almost all of two weeks before the strain of being on the road broke up the band. After parting ways, band members began collaborating separately with manager Malcolm McLaren on the soundtrack to the Julien Temple–directed mockumentary, *The Great Rock 'n' Roll Swindle*, based loosely on the band's history from McLaren's incredibly self-serving point of view. Then of course, there was the incident of October 12, 1978, where Sid might or might not have murdered Nancy. But Sid's demise had been coming for some time.

When those who knew Sid Vicious spoke of his downfall, they would usually point to one of two women: his girlfriend, Nancy Spungen, or his mum, Anne Beverley. Nancy was more maternal than a girlfriend *should* be. And Anne was more affectionately dependent than a *mother* should be.

Sid was suspected of killing one of these women. And the other woman is suspected of killing him.

Sid's Sex Pistols bandmate Johnny Rotten said that Sid was "fucked from the beginning."

"The poor fucker was doomed…His mother was a registered heroin addict, so where do you really go from it?…When parents do that to you, it sets you off on such a fucking bad trip."

Before he was "Sid Vicious," he was Simon John Ritchie, born on May 10, 1957, to a high school dropout for a mom and Buckingham Palace guard/part-time trombone player for a dad. The dream was for the Ritchies to split from the hardscrabble grind of postwar London for an easier way of life in Ibiza, Spain. So young Sid and his mom departed for the Spanish island off the coast of Valencia and waited for Sid's dad to arrive to support the family. He never came. Sid and his mom were forced to return to London to make a life for themselves on their own. It was London in the '60s. Career opportunities for a high school dropout were scarce. Unemployment was on the rise. So, Anne Beverley, in an effort to raise her son by whatever means necessary, took up a heroin habit to obtain free housing for herself and her son from the UK's welfare system. No matter what any heroin addict says about a practical reason to start using, there is never a practical reason that isn't eventually eclipsed by the need to chase the selfish feeling of achieving that very first high again. It's a very warm stone that turns its users into liars with astonishing speed. Worse than becoming a user, Anne Beverley sold drugs to make ends meet. Even worse than that, she was not averse to getting her young son in on the action, sticking a brick of hash down Sid's pants to sneak through customs after a trip to Ibiza. On Sid's sweet sixteen, his mum gave him a little bag of smack and a couple of needles. It took the impressionable young boy little time to reason that if smack filled the hole in his mum's heart, it would probably work for him, too.

Johnny Rotten was right—Sid never had a chance.

And if Anne Beverley's horrible maternal influence on young Sid Vicious wasn't enough, by his twentieth birthday, Nancy Spungen was bulleting down the double barrel of dependency and affection straight toward Sid, who was dead set in her crosshairs.

Nancy Spungen was the alpha dog of 1970s groupies. She was an American heat-seeking missile of a woman who kept time with members of Aerosmith and the Ramones. Her only ambition: to live fast and fuck rock stars. Plan A was Jerry Nolan from the New York Dolls, and in early March 1977, a few days after her nineteenth birthday, Nancy bought a one-way ticket from NYC to London, to follow Nolan and the Dolls on tour. Jerry Nolan wisely gave her the slip. Plan B was Johnny Rotten—who wasn't interested—so Sid was Plan C.

Nancy wasn't one to waste an opportunity. England's newest hitmakers, the Sex Pistols, were making waves in the clubs and on the charts. Nancy, rejected by Nolan and Rotten, quickly moved on to the Pistols' newly minted bassist, Sid Vicious, a decision she based on his looks, his attitude, and his punk rock cred—certainly not on his musical talent.

Sid was hired into the Sex Pistols for the exact same reasons: for everything but his bass chops. By any measure of musicianship, he could barely play his instrument. But that was what made him appealing to Sex Pistols manager Malcolm McLaren. What's more punk than a musician who can't play, was his thinking. The party line for why the band sacked founding member Glen Matlock— writer of many of the Sex Pistols' best songs—was that he had admitted that he liked Paul McCartney. And what's more punk than firing a band member because he admitted to liking a Beatle? Punk's British incarnation was all about dethroning the dinosaurs of rock 'n' roll. Sid hated Paul McCartney. Or so he said. Matlock was out. Sid was in. Manager Malcolm McLaren couldn't have been happier. Sid was a perfect complement to singer Johnny Rotten. An equally disruptive force.

McLaren wanted the Sex Pistols to take the punk attitude further than their American counterparts. The Ramones may have sang that they didn't care about history, but that was bullshit. They covered songs from the '50s and had begun endearing themselves to rock's old guard almost from the jump. When the Sex Pistols performed a cover, they *destroyed* it. Purposefully desecrating rock 'n' roll's sacred cows, doing the unheard of and bailing on the words to Chuck Berry's "Johnny B. Goode," Johnny Rotten prattling on with "I don't know the words, blah blah blah" where the lyrics should have been. He simply didn't care.

And Nancy didn't care about Sid's musicianship, either. He was tabloid famous and punk rock skinny. That was good enough. The pair hit it off immediately. They had a lot in common. She was needy. He was vulnerable. But whereas Sid's shortcomings can easily be traced back to nurture (or lack thereof), Nancy's seemed to be just in her nature. Growing up in a middle-class Philadelphia suburb and raised in a nuclear family, she was highly intelligent— even skipping third grade due to her advanced intellect—but re- gardless, she never really fit in. She was diagnosed as schizophrenic at the age of fifteen, but despite a history of violence her high intelligence continued to open doors for her: She began attending University of Colorado Boulder at the age of sixteen. However, because of her erratic behavior, she would often slam shut all the doors of opportunity that opened for her. Her freshman year in college was marked by a drug bust, an arrest for storing stolen goods in her dorm room. When she was finally expelled, she moved back to the East Coast and began dealing drugs, turning tricks, and stripping before she found her real kicks—hooking up with touring bands and bringing them back to her parents' house for some parental-rattling sex and a homemade breakfast. Notches on her bedpost included Tom Hamilton and Brad Whitford of Aerosmith, Iggy Pop, Richard Hell, and all of the members of the formative version of the New York Dolls except Arthur Kane. Nancy lived hard.

So did Sid Vicious, but Sid's hard-living rock-star status aside, he was fragile—damaged, no doubt, by being brought up by a needy, junkie mum. That fragility carried into Sid's young adulthood, when he met Nancy. Sid was just a few months shy of twenty but was still very much a little boy at heart. Despite the caricatures they would become, the couple really loved one other. Sure, Sid was punk as fuck—on- and offstage—but given a choice, he'd rather sit around in his underwear with Nancy, eat Cheerios, get high, and watch cartoons. And Nancy, for her part, train wreck that she was, really did care for Sid. She looked after him and made sure he didn't shoot too much dope, and she minded his career as best she could. In general, she couldn't stand being away from him.

But both craved attention and both had a taste for violence: violence aimed at both themselves *and* others; cutting themselves out of boredom and quick to enter into public spats physically, usually for show rather than for any real slight.

Sid once told an interviewer, "When I get so annoyed over something, I need an enemy, somebody who's done something to me so that I can take it out on them and beat them to a pulp. And I always find I'm sitting in a room with a load of friends and I can't do anything to them, so I just go upstairs and smash a glass and cut myself. Then I feel better."

And the drugs made all of the violence so much more intense.

Sid and Nancy are often cast as a punk rock version of Romeo and Juliet, star-crossed lovers living fast in leather, dying young, and leaving behind good-looking corpses. But only one of Shakespeare's archetypal lovers willfully ingested poison—and did it only once—whereas Sid and Nancy spent years pumping themselves full of chemicals that should have killed them time and time again.

Nancy began shooting up while still in high school, and though Sid had flirted with the stuff before he met her—thanks to dear ol' mum—from the moment they began their relationship to the bloodied end nineteen months later, smack was the glue that held them together, though many forces would try to pull them apart.

Sid's friend, Motörhead frontman Lemmy Kilmister, said of Sid's relationship, "He never had a chance, ya know. I mean, especially after Nancy got ahold of him, he was over."

This from Mr. Hard As Nails, Lemmy Kilmister: 49 percent motherfucker, 51 percent son of a bitch. A guy who, when a doctor told him his daily intake of Jack and Cokes could kill him, thought the healthiest decision was to switch to screwdrivers because the orange juice provided some vitamin C.

Lemmy wasn't the only one who thought Nancy was too dangerous for Sid.

Sex Pistols manager Malcolm McLaren felt so strongly about it that he tried unsuccessfully to have Nancy run over with a car. He also tried to kidnap her and put her on a plane back to New York. McLaren hated her influence on Sid so much that it was one of the chief reasons he sent the Sex Pistols on tour to America in 1978. Getting Sid away from heroin was McLaren's secondary reason.

While on tour, and without a regular dope supply from his junkie girlfriend, Sid, during a moment of desperation, carved "Gimme a

Young Sid Vicious, drug mule for his mum.

Fix" on his chest with a knife. Beyond Sid's cutting, the tour was a mess. The Sex Pistols, a band with Day-Glo hair and funny accents who spit on their audience, and played a loud, fast, and obnoxious new form of rock 'n' roll that had only recently started to be called punk, went over like a bomb in clubs across the American South. Chaos ensued, and they made headlines everywhere. "Cash for chaos," as McLaren, ever the impresario, gleefully put it.

McLaren intentionally snubbed major American markets like New York and Los Angeles, places where the Pistols would unequivocally be well received, rather than gawked at like sideshow curiosities. The names of the venues alone read like a McLaren punch line: Randy's Rodeo, the Kingfish, the Longhorn Ballroom. This ensured mutual antagonism between the band and audiences. The promotional opportunities were also ridiculous: radio interviews where they were promised leather jackets; regional reporters who didn't get it tagging along. Because they were managed so horribly, the band behaved horribly. Sid disappeared multiple times.

The pressure of it all was too much, and the Sex Pistols disbanded after less than two weeks on the road.

Sid hightailed it back to London to be with Nancy, where they were able to devote all of their energy—and all of the money Sid made on the road—to finding and doing heroin.

Sid and Nancy moved into an unfurnished flat. Elvis Presley had recently died, and radio was milking the King's catalog. His version of Frank Sinatra's "My Way" came on. Sid laughed at its pomp and at the King in general.

"Elvis was cool," Nancy admonished. "Punks wouldn't know shit without the King."

Nancy loved Elvis. Sid thought, maybe Elvis was cool, after all.

Nancy went as far as to suggest to Sid that he should cover Elvis's version of Frank Sinatra's song himself.

Sid could do it *his* way, he thought. Screaming guitars. Feedback. Sid singing it with a snarl that would make Johnny Rotten jealous. Not a bad idea after all. Sid used McLaren's soundtrack for *The Great Rock 'n' Roll Swindle* as an excuse to get into the studio and get the track down. The results were stellar. A completely refreshing take on a track that heretofore had been voiced only by musical giants. Sid had added his own touch to their greatness with ease. The song went to No. 7 on the charts and outsold anything previously recorded by the Sex Pistols. But despite Sid's seeming ascent, the dangerous lifestyle he was living was no secret.

As one reviewer from *NME* remarked, "Just a thought: The last person to record 'My Way' died soon after."

Dying wasn't an option. Not yet, anyway. Sid's solo career was now a priority: second to shooting dope, but still a priority. The "My Way" cover was Nancy's idea. And it was a good one. So in a drug-induced flash of inspiration it was decided: Nancy would be Sid's manager.

There is a lot of footage of the couple during this time: Sitting around in their underwear, nodding off, making out. As artist-manager relationships go, it's highly unusual. But for a couple of full-blown junkies it's standard fare. Sid grew more and more dependent on Nancy's care.

But Sid didn't lack for female attention. His mum was always around, expressing her love for Sid as only she knew how. She'd come by their flat, delivering care packages of jujubes and syringes. As mother-son relationships go, this too was highly unusual. But again, for full-blown junkies, totally standard fare.

However, London was becoming a drag. Maybe it was the lack of excitement now that the Pistols were broken up. Maybe it was the friend who they were considering as a producer who turned up dead in their apartment.

It had started innocently enough: as a business meeting between

Sid, Nancy, and John Shepcock. But no business meeting for the couple was complete without a little powder of some sort, and Sid and Nancy had built up so much of a tolerance for most drugs that mere mortals who tried keeping up with them flirted with death. The couple shared a bed with Shepcock that night, and didn't realize he was dead for several hours into the morning. It almost shocked them into shaping up. Almost.

In any event, it was a catalyst to get the hell out of England. As was, from Nancy's perspective, the smothering presence of Sid's mum. The junkie care packages were one thing, but lately it felt like she was coming by too much, just to make sure the pair were still alive, and to make sure Nancy was doing an adequate job mothering her son. How can a mother who once used her son as a drug mule judge anybody else for not providing adequate care?

Whatever the reason, Sid's solo career needed tending to, and the States seemed like the place to be. But this time Sid would be introduced to the America that wanted him. Sid and Nancy took off for Manhattan. The West Side. To be precise, the Chelsea Hotel.

In 1978, the Chelsea Hotel was already legend. It was where Andy Warhol shot *Chelsea Girls*. Bob Dylan wrote much of *Blonde on Blonde* there. Leonard Cohen wrote "Chelsea Hotel No. 2" about the time he ran into Janis Joplin in the elevator and later woke up next to her in bed. It's where Sam Shepard convinced Patti Smith he was single—and a drummer in a punk band—so that she would sleep with him. Chelsea Guitars was down the block. Mother's was across the street. Lou Reed lived around the corner, and Max's Kansas City was a short cab ride away. For Sid and Nancy, the Chelsea Hotel was the place to be.

They lived on the first floor, aka the "junkies floor," in room 100, the room where Nancy Spungen would die.

Getting ahead in the music industry is tough stuff. Getting ahead in the music industry with a two-gram-a-day habit and a hotel

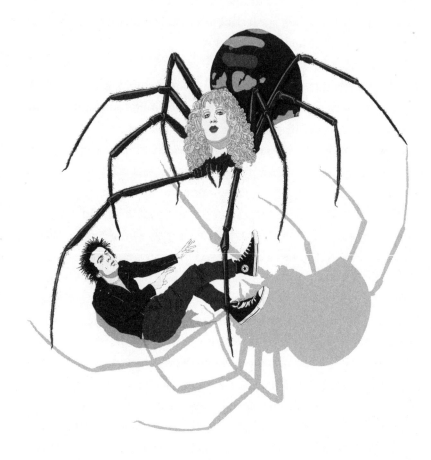

Sid and Nancy.

tan is brutal—so having a dependable supply of smack nearby was clutch.

Nancy quickly began to make strides managing Sid. By September of '78 she had a string of high-paying East Coast gigs lined up at $3,000 to $4,000 a pop. Sid's solo band was hot shit; Mick Jones from the Clash was on guitar, and the New York Dolls rhythm section was enlisted, which meant Nancy's former obsession, Jerry Nolan, would be along for the ride as well.

Sid didn't mind, though. He and Nancy had a different kind of love by now. It was postsexual. More maternal than *en fuego*. Jealousy didn't enter into the equation. Sex was boring. Heroin was God. Music was a means to an end: cash for much-needed dope. Jerry Nolan could come along. At the end of the night, Sid would be nodded out at Nancy's side no matter what.

The gigs paid off. Nancy was flush.

But scoring heroin in New York City was getting harder. Sid sometimes had to head uptown into more dangerous, less known territory and deal with the tremendously sketchy addicts along the way in order to cop. Getting stabbed to death in search of dope in a bad section of town was a very likely but unfortunate prospect for Sid.

Nancy loved Sid. The last thing she wanted was for him to get stabbed scoring dope. So on October 10, 1978, she bought him a Jaguar K-11 knife for protection. It had a five-inch blade on it. And that blade would end up in her stomach within a number of hours.

There was no dramatic precursor to Nancy Spungen's murder. Relatively speaking, anyway. There was no fight. No breakdown. Nothing hinting at premeditation. Sid and Nancy were in love— their own version of love, sure, but love nonetheless. They needed each other like a needle needs a spoon. With Nancy minding Sid's career there was at least some sort of professional horizon to look out onto after waking up from dope binges. And despite the current state of available heroin, Mr. and Mrs. Too Stoned to Fuck were settled into their own routine, their own version of domestic bliss.

So like any other normal couple in the throes of love, they decided to throw a party in their room at the Chelsea. Except Sid and Nancy weren't a normal couple. And this was the Chelsea Hotel.

Friends shuffled in and out. The main point of their visits was so Nancy could score junk. She and Sid were hurting and on the verge of withdrawal. Nancy had called everyone looking for smack. No dice. The best she could do was convince her friend Rockets Redglare to come by with some synthetic morphine. The scene was dark. Unable to score dope, Sid had downed thirty Tuinals and couldn't move. Nancy kept the guests coming in, friends with drugs to spare, and a few dealers, but nobody had any heroin. The party broke up. Sid roamed the halls looking for a fix. Nothing. Back to the room.

He and Nancy were alone. The pain was all-consuming. The pills and booze added a haze but did little to numb the hurt. Sid felt it the worst. They tried soothing each other. On their bed they were a tangled junkie mess. In each other's arms, taking turns moaning in agony in between barely audible mumbles. Sid faded in and out of consciousness.

Their death pact was on Sid's mind. The one where they'd promised to kill themselves if the other had died, so that they could be buried next to each other in their leather jackets, jeans, and motorcycle boots. The pact would always come up in moments like these: when the pain got to be too much. Sid sweating it out. Mumbling incoherently. Nancy jabbering on and on.

"We should've gone uptown earlier to score when we had the chance."

"Where the fuck was Rockets Redglare with those pills?"

"Jerry Nolan always had dope…"

"This was somehow all that cunt Malcolm McLaren's fault."

She wouldn't shut up. Words, words…more words. Sid came to. They lay face-to-face still twisted up in pain. Sid was shirtless. "Gimme a Fix" scarred across his chest. Black jeans. Half-inch bike chain and lock around his neck. There was the pain again. And there was his knife. He'd had it in his pocket or in his hand ever since Nancy had given it to him the day before. She was jonesing hard now. Sweating in just her black panties and bra. Near naked. Talking nonstop. She would not shut up.

Kill Me Now…

Gimme a Fix…

Sleep Forever…

No More Pain…

Sid couldn't think straight. Words. Just words. More words. Sid did his best but he understood little beyond the pain.

Deep. Agonizing pain.

Nancy was pissed. More words. The tangle turned to a tussle. There was the knife. Pain. Sharp pain.

No more words.

Silence.

When Sid Vicious awoke he found the love of his life, Nancy Spungen, dead on their bathroom floor. Her body crammed between the toilet and the sink in an upright position. Blood covered her knees and legs. Her knees, perpetually scarred, were not the source of the blood, though. It was the single stab wound in her abdomen—just below her belly button—from the five-inch blade of Sid's knife.

"I stabbed her, but I didn't mean to kill her," he told police at one point. "I loved her, but she treated me like shit."

That sounded like a lot of smack.

Again it was the sign. The sign that said, YOU ARE NOW EXITING RIKERS ISLAND PRISON COMPLEX, but what Sid saw was a sign that said, YOU ARE NOW ABOUT TO GET HIGH AS FUCK.

Because he'd just made bail. His mum and his friend, Peter Kodick, were waiting for him. They'd arranged it so the first order of business was getting him high. Then there was to be a party for him. And tomorrow, he was supposed to get around to seeing that famous lawyer, F. Lee Bailey, that Mick Jagger had been secretly and generously paying for. *Mick Jagger? Shit.*

That was what Sid Vicious was likely thinking on the first day of February 1979, when he left Rikers Island prison, the first day of the rest of his life, that would only last—roughly—another eighteen hours.

In prison for seven weeks, Sid straightened out. Sobriety begot clarity, and with clarity the ghost of Nancy came knocking. Sid was still reeling from the uncertainty of whether or not he did or didn't kill the love of his life.

Imagine that: You wake up dazed from horse tranquilizers and your girlfriend, your soulmate, your best friend, your business manager—hell, let's be real, the only woman who *truly* mothered you—is lying dead on your floor. You don't *think* you killed her. I mean, why would you? You depended on her. You needed her. You loved her. When you were upset, you'd nurse at her breast. She'd call you "baby boy" and you'd call her "Momma." Her death—and your uncertainty—haunted you.

Did you do it?

Did you kill her?

How could you do it?

How could you kill her?

Did you do it to end her pain? Nancy was always talking about her pain. The pain you helped dull with the love you showed her.

Love. What was love besides a barometer to measure your pain against? The pain that had been with you since childhood. The loneliness. The distrust of anyone not named "Mum" or, later, "Nancy." But death? Death had potential. A potential cure for pain. Heroin was a temporary fix. Death was where it was at.

You said you'd die with her. Happily. She agreed, and so the death pact was real. Wasn't it? Or was it just something you talked about when the dope sickness got to be too painful?

Was it?

Or wasn't it?

In times of inescapable emptiness after Nancy's death, Sid had tried to kill himself, but it never took. He took all of his methadone supply at once. No luck. He tried to slash his wrists, but that didn't work, either. Then it was suicide by way of a Hell's Kitchen bar fight but that just landed him back in Rikers.

He wrote to Nancy's mother: "Every day is agony without her. I know now that it is possible to die from a broken heart. Because when you love someone as much as we love each other, they become fundamental to your existence. So I will die soon, even if I don't kill myself. I guess you could say that I'm pining for her. I could live without food or water longer than I'm going to survive without Nancy."

With Nancy on his mind, Sid was eager to reunite with the other love of his life, heroin.

The party that was planned was small but spirited. It would be at the Village apartment of his new girlfriend, Michelle Robinson, who was the methadone version of Nancy. A brunette, she could pass for a sister of Nancy's, sharing the physical resemblance through the nose and eyes, but she didn't command a room—or Sid's heart—the way that his dead lover did. Michelle had invited Peter Kodick, Jerry Only from the Misfits, a handful of other yea-sayers, and Sid's mum, who was busy fixing one off for Sid. His first shot of heroin after seven weeks of detox in Rikers.

Sid's mum had been the worst of influences since he was in short pants. But now, her shitty parenting wasn't the problem. Her shitty dope was. Sid injected it, but nothing. He was furious. Peter Kodick was dispatched to the streets to find real heroin.

Kodick scored. And *his* dope did the trick. Sid nearly OD'd. His friends revived him, but the party died out.

Dope addicts know that the first hit after detox can be fatal. The trick is injecting the perfect amount. Balancing enough to get high, but not enough to shock your system to death. That was what happened when Sid booted up that first time out of prison. Too much dope. Too much good dope, to be exact. He wanted more but was too high to shoot himself up. He asked his girlfriend to do it, but nuh-uh. She'd seen enough of this junkie hari-kari.

So Sid's mum, Anne Beverley, entered the apartment bedroom where her son was sprawled out in need of a fix, sometime in the early morning hours of February 2, 1979. For Sid, the heroin numbed the pain. The pain of missing Nancy. The pain of not knowing whether or not he killed her.

Kill me now…

He needed more. That was why Mum was there. So much pain. Lying alone in a strange bed. Thinking of Nancy.

Was *she* there?

Was she dead?

Was this all a dream?

Were they back at the Chelsea? Was he gone already? Where was he going? In and out of consciousness.

There. Then gone. Then back…with the pain.

Gimme a fix…

He felt warm hands on his arms. Affectionately tying him off and rooting around for a vein. Were they his mother's hands? Or Nancy's? Maybe it was the hand of God, for all Sid knew. Either way, it was a touch he'd grown to depend on. Then, a pinprick.

Maybe this dope would do the trick. Maybe *it* would do what the slitting of the wrists and the Hell's Kitchen beating couldn't do: end the pain.

He was drifting. He could hear singing. It was faint in his ear. It was the song that his mum used to sing to him as a little boy, after his dad left them stranded in Ibiza. It didn't matter. He and his mum had each other. It never seemed like enough for her, but for a time it was all Sid needed. It sounded so sweet to hear her craggy British voice singing along with the soulful American man on the radio. What was that guy's name? Sam something. His mum used to sing a bunch of his songs.

And I know that if you love me, too
What a wonderful world this would be.

This dope was *so* heavy. Nancy was definitely there with him now. Or was it Mum? It had to be Nancy. She was always there when the pain got to be too much. She was holding Sid's head to her bosom. Rocking him back and forth gently. Speaking to him softly. Words. Baby boy…Momma…Just words. Pain. Drifting pain.

And then…

Sleep.

Forever.

Sid was dead.

The official cause of death; heroin overdose.

The unofficial cause of death? Suicide by heroin.

The *rumored* cause of death? Sid's mum gave him a hotshot.

Why? A maternal act of mercy. In 1996, before her own deadly overdose, Anne Beverley supposedly confessed to journalist Alan Parker that she had indeed given her son his final dose of heroin. Accounts from that night align with that confession.

Anne Beverley was a lifelong, experienced heroin addict who knew exactly how much dope a person could handle if they had been clean for seven weeks. And, more important, she knew exactly how much dope it would take to kill a person if they had been clean for seven weeks. There is no way she couldn't have known.

But why exactly?

Sid beating Nancy's murder rap was a long shot. Rikers, with its rapists and real punks, terrified Sid. So did Nancy's ghost. Doing twenty-plus years was unimaginable for the fragile rock star. He was suicidal. And Anne could finally take care of him the way a mother should.

She was still singing to him, though she knew he was probably gone now. But if he could hear her as he drifted away, she wanted him to feel safe, to feel loved.

And I know that if you love me, too
What a wonderful world this would be.

CHAPTER 8

SAM COOKE

SAM COOKE PUSHED THE WORRIES to the back of his mind and pulled his Ferrari into Lou Rawls's driveway. A visit with his old friend Lou would be good for his soul. Sam knew Lou from way back. Two decades slinging the gospel at the tops of their lungs throughout Chicago's South Side churches will bond you to a fellow. You can hear that bond and the ease of their relationship in Lou's effortless harmony in the call-and-response chorus of Sam's 1962 classic, "Bring It on Home to Me."

Lou's six-month-old son began crying upon Sam's arrival. Sam loved babies, but Little Lou Rawls Jr. was having none of him and Sam, in return, was getting emotional around the little dude. The next week would have been the third birthday of Sam's own son, Vincent, who had drowned in the family swimming pool the year before. The death put an increased strain on what was already a strained relationship with his wife, and led Sam on a path of recklessness.

Nineteen sixty-four was tough on Sam. But it was also productive. It had been his most prolific as a songwriter and in a lot of ways his most rewarding creatively as he began turning his pop craftsmanship to more serious social issues. After hearing Bob

Dylan's "Blowin' in the Wind," just two months after his son died, Sam realized the answer wasn't blowin' in the wind at all, but the answer was inside *him*. Just sitting there. Waiting to be exorcised and unleashed onto the world. So Sam wrote, "A Change Is Gonna Come." It was a less esoteric, more contemporary take on what Dylan had done with "Blowin' in the Wind." It was a direct claim on the happiness that eluded black America and his audience. It was unabashedly hopeful. Nearly sentimental but completely devoid of cheese. It was also Sam taking a swing at reclaiming some personal happiness for himself after the death of his son. And America loved it.

The baby wouldn't stop wailing.

Sam picked up Lou Jr., playfully looked the crying infant in his eyes, and asked, "What's the matter with you, man?"

Sam tried humming "Wonderful World." It was the song that had earned him his nickname of Mr. Wonderful, and it usually did the trick. Women, babies, didn't matter. Sam's voice could fix most anyone's problems. But not today. Lou put his son in his room, and the two old friends retired to the living room.

Sam Cooke and Lou Rawls met before they were even teenagers, forming a quartet and singing doo-wop on street corners in Chicago. They both joined a gospel group called the Highway QC's. The QC's were onto something but were not going anywhere fast enough for Sam, so he joined the Soul Stirrers at the age of nineteen. The Soul Stirrers were well established. They'd been slinging it on the gospel circuit since 1926, before Sam was born. The group's members were immensely talented, but Sam had a unique and natural gift all his own. Sex appeal, though subversive, was always part of gospel performance, but Sam Cooke brought a different kind of sexuality to it; it was subtle, less suggestive, more sophisticated. It was innate and as effortless as his uniquely intimate style of singing.

And his singing style was indeed unique. It wasn't like what other gospel singers brought to the game. It wasn't all emotion. It wasn't all truth. Like Frank Sinatra, Sam's voice transcended style. It transcended technique, and it effortlessly balanced vulnerability and authority. Like Cupid's arrow, Sam Cooke's voice was a shot to the heart. And it made him irresistible.

Irresistible to record executives who saw in Sam a crossover into secular pop music and who wanted a big payday. Irresistible to seasoned musicians who knew a special talent when they saw it and wanted to go along for the ride. Irresistible to young black men who saw a successful artist and businessman who they wanted to be. And irresistible to women who just wanted him.

Lots and lots of women wanted Sam Cooke.

Forget Cupid's arrow. With that voice, Sam Cooke might as well have been Cupid himself.

When Sam was in the room, you felt his sexuality. Mavis Staples referred to him as "Sam the Seducer." Back in the Soul Stirrer days, Sam hadn't quite graduated to bespoke suits yet, but he dressed impeccably and had that tight, processed hair. He kept himself looking good and out on tour as a Soul Stirrer; Sam was as much a sexual conquistador as he was a gospel missionary.

There were women in every town. Either waiting for him or waiting to meet him for the first time. Old girls. New girls. Black girls. White girls. Sam referred to white women as "snow" and sleeping with black women as, quote, "shoveling coal."

It was a well-developed circuit. One that to a young man must have seemed bountiless. And unwanted pregnancies? Well, that was just the cost of doing business. By the time Sam was twenty-one, he'd had three children with three different women.

But it didn't matter. He was Teflon. The out-of-wedlock pregnancies and rep didn't stick. His image remained squeaky clean.

If that nice boy next door with the wide smile and polite manner, the one who keeps himself so clean and sings like an angel, if he wants to sleep with my granddaughter, then better him than that flashy, campaign-shouting Southern diplomat from down on the corner. If it's got to be someone it might as well be Sam Cooke. Or so went the thinking of little old lady churchgoers everywhere.

Understanding the effect Sam Cooke had on people both onstage and off isn't easy. He was good-looking, charming, and immensely talented but beyond that, he legitimately had that "thing." The little extra something that is elusive, impossible to describe, and contributes to one's star quality. Sam Cooke had it. And onstage, particularly in those early days with the Soul Stirrers, "it" was a weapon. To truly understand Sam Cooke's appeal, you have to understand that he learned how to reach people by being a *gospel singer.*

Back when his name was spelled *C-O-O-K,* before he added the *E* at the end for sophistication, before he was topping the pop charts or seen ripping through Hollywood in his cherry red Ferrari or out on the town dressed to kill in a Sy Devore suit, before *that* Sam Cooke, there was Sam Cook. No *E* at the end. The polite son of a Chicago-by-way-of-Mississippi minister. Sam's dad was a fire-and-brimstone country preacher who took his musical family— Sam included, of course—on the road to perform gospel music at various church services throughout the Midwest.

This gospel touring circuit was where Sam Cook started to hone his performance chops. The point of gospel music might have been to celebrate the Lord, but the point of gospel *performance* was to captivate the audience and vanquish all rivals. Gospel performers were highly competitive. And they had to be. The amount of talent within the scene was astounding; the Five Blind Boys of Mississippi, Mahalia Jackson, and the group Sam Cooke would one day join and lead, the Soul Stirrers, all shared immense gifts.

So Sam knew how to get to people *on a spiritual level* by using all his God-given gifts to shake you to your core and hold you. You were enraptured. You were powerless against his charms. And because of this, Sam Cooke—aka Mr. Wonderful, aka Cupid, aka Sam the Seducer, aka the man with the golden tongue and the unbridled libido—grew very accustomed to getting exactly what he wanted whenever he wanted it.

Sam had gotten what he wanted, all right. A shot at the big time. It wasn't easy, but he was able to navigate his way out of the gospel scene and for the most part avoid the dreaded "sellout" rap. His first single, *his first single*, "You Send Me," went to No. 1 on the pop charts. Not just the R&B charts. *The top of the pop charts.*

And getting to the top sometimes seemed like a giant pain in the ass, but it was worth the sweat. Success was indeed sweet. And Sam deserved it. He was special and he knew it. When most of his peers were blowing their bread willy-nilly, Sam was investing in himself.

He founded his own record label, SAR, and was writing and producing and giving younger soul musicians on the come-up a shot. And his new manager, the very astute Allen Klein, had just swung a deal with RCA Records, where Sam Cooke, a black man in 1964 America, would own SAR's master recordings. This was a big deal. It meant power in the music industry. An industry that, in the early 1960s, was entirely controlled by white men and gangster con artists whose record labels distributed their music through a national syndicate of mafia-controlled jukeboxes and who relied on the mob to employ a network of crooked radio promo men to bribe DJs to play their records on the airwaves and thus increase record sales and generate profit from the exploitation of the master recordings owned by the labels and the publishers. Now Sam Cooke owned the master recordings. And the label. This was not only rare for a black musician at the time, it was rare for any musician. Still is, actually.

Sam Cooke—a black man and a *real* artist—was also an executive producer who controlled his own future and was able to provide real opportunities for young black men and support, with both his voice and his wallet, the growing civil rights movement.

It had been a long time coming for sure, but change—in some ways—had come. Sam had come a long way from selling "race records" out of barbershops and shoe-shine stands to hanging with Muhammad Ali and headlining the Copa.

And now, a stable of younger artists depended on him for guidance, material, expertise, and tour and financial support. Plus, his own career still needed minding.

He complained to Lou about the pressure. Lou Jr. was still screaming in his bedroom, and the screams were pressing down on Sam's last nerve.

"Hey Lou, what do you say we get out of here? I've got dinner with Al, and I'm gonna meet some radio folks at P.J.'s later."

P.J.'s in West Hollywood was dark, intimate, and cozy. A place where dudes like Sam Cooke—super-charismatic and famous pop singers—could hang unnoticed and largely be left alone. Al Schmitt was his trusted engineer, who had helmed such Sam Cooke hits as "Another Saturday Night," "Cupid," and the aforementioned "Bring It on Home to Me." And Sam wanted to meet with the KAPP DJs at the local R&B station to ensure they were on board for his ambitious next release.

Sam's current album for RCA, *Ain't That Good News*, was ending its cycle, and he had plans for his greatest creative achievement yet: a blues album that perfectly melded his patented sophisticated soul with the down-home gut punch of blues artists he loved, like John Lee Hooker and Muddy Waters. It was unclear how Sam was going to pull this off but he was obsessed.

As he always did, he asked Lou what he thought. Lou knew that Sam didn't really need his input, but he dug that his famous friend still solicited his advice. Sam, however, needed Lou more than the man knew. Finding the space to think and be creative was not easy for Sam. There was always something. The investment in himself? It was paying off but, man, it was stressful sometimes. He hoped Lou would come with him for a few drinks, but Lou was worried that Lou Jr. was sick, and leaving a sick six-month-old with the missus would not bode well in the long run.

Sam could understand Lou wanting to be cautious with his wife. Sam hadn't been very cautious with his own. He'd married Barbara Campbell, the mother of one of his six children, thinking marriage would add a sense of order to his life, but all it did was add more chaos. The home, despite the wall-to-wall carpet, the brand-new hi-fi, and the pool out back, was a straight-up battlefield when Barbara was around. That woman was almost as restless as he was. The tension was thick and ever present.

And the goddamn phone? It never stopped ringing.

The Valentinos' bus had broken down out on tour.

Little Billy Preston needed money for a new organ.

Johnnie Taylor was pissed off again about something or another.

And Martin was calling. He wanted to talk to Sam about performing at a benefit for the Southern Christian Leadership Conference early next year.

Sam would do anything for Martin Luther King Jr., but right now the civil rights movement would have to wait. Sam needed to blow off some steam and get his head right.

Lou could stay home with his sick baby. Sam needed some action.

Sam Cooke's Ferrari hit the valet at Martoni's in Hollywood sometime on the evening of December 10, 1964. He'd meant to get dinner at P.J.'s with Al and his wife, but when he saw the babe at the Martoni's bar, he got up, bailed on going to dinner with Mr. and Mrs. Al, and casually approached the woman who had caught his eye. She was no astronaut's wife, but she'd do.

Sam Cooke, singer, soul man, activist, Mr. Wonderful.

At the bar, though, Sam was swarmed by friends and hangers-on. The drinks were flowing, and Sam was leading the bar in sing-along after sing-along until the woman he had his eye on started making eyes at him, demanding his attention. Sam was at her side in no time with a drink. She was just his type. And of course, he was hers. With Sam's energy now focused on the task at hand, the vibe at the bar died down. A change of scenery was needed, so they decided to hit P.J.'s over on Santa Monica.

Now after midnight, Sam was at least four or five martinis deep. Little Miss Thing had a name: Elisa Boyer. As closing time approached, she was approaching something near stunning to Sam, and she was garnering attention from other men at P.J.'s besides himself. Mr. Wonderful grew angry. A fight nearly ensued.

Fuck the bars, he thought. Let's get some privacy.

The two jumped in Sam's Ferrari and were out on the 405 in no time.

He was driving fast. Heading out of town. Where were they going? Elisa was staying downtown. Don't worry about none of that, Sam remarked.

Relax.

Enjoy the ride.

He turned on the radio, KAPP. Shit! Sam realized he had forgotten to meet up with those DJs earlier in the night. Frustrated, he twirled the dial from KAPP and landed on the sounds of Elvis Presley's "Blue Christmas." He left it and let Elvis's baritone ring out. He was too distracted by Elisa sitting to his right.

And Elisa was worried. She told Sam she wanted to get out of the car. He was clearly drunk. Driving like a lunatic. Pulling off a bottle of scotch. And apparently headed somewhere out by the airport. She had no idea where.

But Sam had an idea. The Hacienda Motel. It was perfect.

Remote. Quiet. Cheap. And indiscriminate of color or marital status. No last-call lotharios to loosen the vibe while trying to get Little Miss Strange to help him blow off his steam.

But Elisa seriously wasn't having it.

It didn't matter. She'd come around. They always did. He was Sam Cooke. Mr. Fucking Wonderful.

The Ferrari sloppily roared into the Hacienda parking lot at 2:35 a.m. Sam hit the motel manager's office looking like a damn fool. Wild-eyed. Anxious. Drunk. To the motel manager, he looked exactly like every other man who checked in at two in the morning. She gave him a room key and noticed the girl in the Ferrari with the Jacqueline Kennedy scarf and glasses. She made Sam sign in as part of a married couple. He couldn't remember Elisa's name, so he just wrote "Mr. and Mrs. Sam Cooke."

In the motel room, things were not going as Sam planned. Elisa, despite her googly-eyed bullshit back at the bar, wasn't picking up what Sam was putting down.

Sam had had enough. He was impatient. Horny. He grabbed her. Groping. Kissing.

All hands.

No heart.

Gone was the subtlety he was known for onstage and in records. It was replaced by a base, carnal desire that was obvious and boring. The same as all of the other ordinary men she'd known.

Elisa was disgusted. Wanted no part of it. What she wanted was for Sam to take her home. Now.

But Sam had never been denied before, and he couldn't imagine a world where a woman wouldn't want to be with him. What a nonwonderful world that would be. He was gonna have it his way or nothing at all.

She'd come around. They always did. He was *the* Sam Cooke. Executive Seducer. It was only a matter of time. Besides...he had to piss. He'd hit the bathroom to give Little Miss Strange a minute to collect herself.

Instead, she collected her clothes and got the fuck out of there. In a hurry.

She split. Ran out of the room half-naked, in just her bra and slip, and through the parking lot, past the motel manager's office, and out onto the street. And just like that? Gone. In the wind.

Sam came out of the bathroom to an empty room. No strange. The door was open. Sam was naked. And his clothes were gone…And his wallet? What the fuck.

He grabbed all he could find: his blazer and one shoe. Scooped up his car keys, jumped in the Ferrari, and squealed over to the manager's office where he imagined Elisa to be hiding out. Again, he parked like an asshole, jumped out of the car. Left the driver's side door open and with one shoe on and with little Sam Cooke hanging out beneath his blazer, he began pounding on the door.

"Let me in! Where is she?

"Where are my clothes? She *took* my wallet!"

On the other side of the door was fifty-five-year-old Bertha Lee Franklin. She'd checked Sam in earlier and knew exactly how fucked-up the fool on the other side of the door was. She was nonplussed. And was on the phone with her boss at the moment as she always was at this time of night.

So she ignored Sam.

Sam grew more upset and started shouting again.

"She ain't in here."

"Yes she is! I know she is. Let me in!"

"Mister, there ain't no one in here but me."

That was when Sam started ramming the door with his shoulder. Three tries and he came pouring into the joint like a bag of banged-up bricks.

Bertha Lee was stunned. Still on the phone, she told this naked fool to get out. That the woman he was looking for wasn't there. But Sam, cockblocked and blueballed, was not hearing it. He was leering over her shoulder into the apartment adjacent to the motel manager's office—he knew she was in there, and he now thought that this woman was in on whatever scam was being run on him. After all, why the hell else wouldn't that woman want to sleep with him?

"Where the fuck is she? And where are my clothes?"

"Mister, she ain't here. You gotta go."

Sam snapped. He grabbed Bertha Lee by the shoulders and started shaking her. The struggle intensified. The phone fell to the floor. Bertha Lee tried biting, scratching…Sam threw her to the ground and pounced…still naked and even more enraged but Bertha Lee was able to get out from under him and wobble to her feet.

She knew where the gun was. It was there for a reason. This reason. To fend off some wild-eyed, horny, drunk fool in the middle of the night. She grabbed the .22 resting on the television, and as Sam started to come at her again she aimed and pulled the trigger.

The first shot whistled over his head.

The second, past his shoulder.

And the third?

Straight into the heart of Cupid.

Stunned, Sam Cooke looked up at Bertha Lee Franklin and said, "Lady, you shot me?"

Sam fell to his knees and for a moment seemed subdued but then, in a last burst of adrenaline, attacked Bertha Lee again. This time would be his last. She could sense that life was a fleeting proposition for this naked fool and showed mercy. She dropped the gun. Grabbed a broom and gave Sam a simple oops upside the head to keep him at bay. It was all that was needed. He fell over and died.

Bertha Lee Franklin shot and killed Sam Cooke. The court cleared her of any charges. The homicide was ruled justifiable.

But the court of public opinion thought otherwise. She received numerous death threats, was forced to quit her job and go into hiding. She was sued by Sam Cooke's widow for her husband's funeral expenses. A husband who was one of the most successful pop stars in the world. A husband she grieved over for exactly three months before marrying his good friend, Bobby Womack.

Still, to this day, the world does not want to accept that Bertha Lee Franklin shot and killed Sam Cooke. Though the circumstances of his death are not shrouded in mystery.

There is no shortage of rock 'n' roll conspiracy theories. They exist in part because fans don't want to let go. There are legions who believe Buddy Holly, Ritchie Valens, and the Big Bopper never crashed and burned in an Iowa cornfield back on February 3, 1959, the supposed "day the music died," and are somehow still alive, making music and living happily ever after. Some even believe that the crash was caused by something nefarious like Buddy Holly firing a pistol inside the plane at the pilot as a means to affect his own suicide. This is a real theory. And people believe it. Just like the people who choose to believe that Rolling Stones guitar player Brian Jones was murdered by Mick Jagger and Keith Richards as a way to get the increasingly strung-out and useless band member out of their lives forever. Which is almost as ridiculous as those who believe that Courtney Love murdered Kurt Cobain because they didn't have a prenup. A small cottage industry has built up around Elvis Presley conspiracy theories. Most fascinating is the theory that Elvis's twin brother, Jesse, did not die at birth; that he lived on and still lives to this day, and that's the reason why there have been so many Elvis sightings since the King's reported death back in 1977. And of course, the granddaddy music conspiracy theory of all time is that Elvis *faked* his own death and does indeed still live on. Why else would he have misspelled his own name on his headstone? This is true. Look it up.

But regardless, Elvis is not alive. Neither is his brother. And Kurt wasn't murdered and the Stones aren't assassins. Buddy didn't pop one off in the back of the pilot's head to crash his plane and Sam Cooke wasn't killed by anyone other than Bertha Lee Franklin.

It wasn't a jilted lover.

It wasn't a jealous husband.

It wasn't a robbery gone wrong.

And it wasn't the mafia.

It was a justifiable homicide. So said the jury.

Sam Cooke, despite the conspiracy theories that sprung up immediately, was not the victim. Bertha Lee Franklin was.

The jury knew this because Bertha Lee voluntarily took and passed a lie detector test. As did her boss, the owner of the hotel, Evelyn Carr, who was on the phone with her at the time the incident went down.

The jury also knew from phone records stating that at 3:15 a.m., as soon as the phone line disconnected and while Sam was attacking Bertha Lee, Evelyn Carr called the police to report what she'd heard on the other end of the motel phone. Of course, the police had a record of that call.

And the call came *minutes* after Elisa Boyer had called the police herself—from a pay phone out on the street from the hotel—to report that she had been *kidnapped*.

Furthermore, as soon as the police arrived on the scene, Elisa emerged from the shadows to voluntarily speak to them about everything that just happened.

There is no mystery surrounding Sam Cooke's death. There is no conspiracy. Mr. Wonderful was denied that night in the Hacienda Hotel, and there was nothing Cupid could do about it.

Sam Cooke, shot dead by the female hotel manager he attacked, half-naked.

CHAPTER 9

LISA "LEFT EYE" LOPES

THE SUIT FROM THE RECORD LABEL was telling Lisa the new single wasn't strong enough, but the playback was telling her something else. *They'd have to test the single out in the overseas market.* What the hell was that all about? Test the single out? Despite what the Suit said, Lisa liked what she heard. The chord progression reminded her of "Bonita Applebum" by A Tribe Called Quest. This shit was dope. Definitely strong enough to be the first single. At the very least, it could be the leadoff track on her solo debut. She smiled, thinking about how it would throw TLC fans for a loop if the first thing they heard from one-third of the best-selling American female group of all time was the voice of a man—and not just the voice of any man; it was the sweet croon of Carl Thomas, whose "woah oh ohhhh" was channeling the same swoops of Sam Cooke's "You Send Me," a song her dad played for her as a kid.

This was so different from anything on the TLC tip. Lisa "Left Eye" Lopes, the spitfire singer for one of the hottest R&B groups of the '90s, loved messing with people's expectations, and now she wanted to show the world how creative she really was. Two years before she had challenged her bandmates to make solo albums, just like she was. Her vision was to release them all as a three-CD set on one day. She encouraged LaFace, the group's label, to choose whose album was best and award the "winner" $1.5 million. To seal the deal, she challenged her bandmates and label by writing an open letter to all parties concerned in *Entertainment Weekly*. It was true to form. Most everything Lisa did was over-the-top.

Her bandmates, T-Boz and Chilli, responded publicly by saying that "Left Eye is only concerned with Left Eye," and "she doesn't respect the whole group." So, no solo albums from the TLC members to compete with. Lisa didn't care. She knew she was going to make a great solo record no matter what. But she didn't.

The album was a bust. It was released overseas at first, and sales were so underwhelming that the label never released it in the United States. That's how poorly the record performed.

Lisa wasn't used to anyone telling her she was performing poorly. *Behaving* poorly? Now that was something she was more accustomed to. But every time she went onstage, she brought it. What was "poorly," anyway? It was all relative. TLC had sold 65 million albums worldwide, so even sales in the single-digit millions would have been deemed a "poorly" selling record by her label.

This business was killing her. People talking shit about her, saying she was crazy, selfish, messed up in the head, etc. They said all that even before she burned down Andre's house.

After the fire was the first time she went to Honduras. A spiritual journey. And now, with her solo album a bust, she needed to get away again, back to her roots, and anchor herself to the rhythm beating inside of her, back to why she did this in the first place: the music.

Lisa "Left Eye" Lopes came from a long line of artists and musicians. From a young age, her natural talent was evident— she sang, wrote, drew, danced. Her dad played piano, clarinet, the harmonica—basically, he could play anything he got his hands on. But, just like with her boyfriend, Andre, her dad's hands were also part of the problem.

Lisa loved her dad, but domestic abuse was always up in the mix. Maybe it had something to do with his fiery creative nature, maybe it was due to his stint in the military—maybe. Most likely it was his drinking.

Lisa's dad was super strict about everything except drinking. In fact, from the time Lisa was a preteen, they bonded over booze. Daddy-daughter days would just as well be a trip to the movies as they would be a drinking competition in the backyard. "Look at Little Lisa get after that beer."

For some musicians, drinking and creativity go hand in hand—often, the one begets the other. For Lisa, her creativity and her drinking were at odds from the jump.

Lisa would joke that when she got too drunk, all of her behavior could be blamed on her alter ego, Nikki.

But despite Nikki's presence causing plenty of trouble during her school days, Lisa's creativity usually won the day.

She acted in school productions, sometimes as the star, sometimes as a backup dancer. She modeled and used her gifts as an illustrator to design her own outfits. Her brain was filled with a million different creative endeavors, each as compelling to her as the next. She wrote poetry and of course rhymes. And rhymes were the ticket to the future.

It was 1990 and hip-hop was exploding, and for a young Lisa Lopes, potentially transformative.

Just up the road in Atlanta, the South's burgeoning hip-hop scene was making waves. Taking its cues from the big bass sounds of Miami "Booty Music" down the road a piece, Atlanta hip-hop was growing into something wholly unique; sweetened melodies contrasted with drawled-out rhymes over big, electro-funk beats. The music lacked the abrasiveness of East Coast rap and eschewed the hardcore reality of gangsta rap out west for something different; a laid-back Southern sophistication that knew instinctively when to deploy maximum R&B to keep the party bumping. Two ambitious local movers and shakers, Antonio "LA" Reid and Kenneth "Baby-face" Edmonds, were busy promoting and producing a wellspring of homegrown talent. Artists like Outkast, Toni Braxton, and Usher were about to bring what would come to be known as the "Dirty South" to middle America.

So in 1990, nineteen-year-old Lisa Lopes hit Atlanta with $750 in her pocket.

When you're nineteen and possessed by creativity, the Universe has a way of making it all just kind of happen. It delicately pushes and pulls and presents you with opportunities. If you're smart, you listen to what the Universe has to say. Lisa Lopes was no dummy.

So when she finally connected with a couple of other Atlanta transplants, she knew that as a trifecta they'd be unstoppable. The name TLC originally came from the three members' names: Tionne Watkins, aka T-Boz, was the *T*, Lisa was the *L*, and a singer, Rozonda Thomas, who assumed the nickname of "Chilli" so the trio could keep their initials intact. They liked the name: it reminded them of the part in Michael Jackson's "PYT (Pretty Young Thing)," where MJ sings "You need some lovin'," and the background singers chime in with "TLC." They'd sometimes sing this to each other in the early days. And older folks would inevitably associate it with Elvis Presley, who came up with a slogan, "Taking Care of Business," and a logo with the initials TCB over a lightning bolt. When Elvis cared about a male friend, he'd give them a TCB necklace. For females, it was a TLC. From time to time somebody would tell this story to the girls of TLC. But this being the '90s, they associated Elvis more with Chuck D's line in "Fight the Power":

Elvis was a hero to most
But he never meant shit to me, you see

Straight up racist, that sucker was
Simple and plain.

Once the definitive lineup of TLC was in place, there was no time to waste. Yeah, T-Boz took her stage name to show she was a boss, but it was Left Eye—with a nickname co-opted from an offhand pickup line fed to her by some dude—who was calling the creative shots.

T-Boz had the voice—sultry, smooth, instantly recognizable. Chilli was the dancer with, it seemed, new moves every damn day of the week. So that left Lisa. She was the wild card. She'd play the crazy one. If the shoe fit...

It didn't matter. She knew she'd stand out in a trio of outstanding talent and style regardless of whatever role she had to play to sell an image and, ultimately, records. And the shoe did fit. With her alter ego Nikki's presence, crazy was something Lisa was well acquainted with. TLC was poised for greatness. Lisa was high on the future.

But TLC was much more than just talent, attitude, and style. Equal parts En Vogue, Salt-N-Pepa, and some sugar-high cartoon that jumped off the back of your little sister's cereal box, TLC were something completely new. TLC was very much of the moment. They tapped into the social consciousness of the decade, promoting safe sex with the style of the MTV generation.

Their first album, *Ooooooohhh...On the TLC Tip*, was released in 1992. They came charging out of the gate with the video for "Ain't 2 Proud 2 Beg": Left Eye with those massive sunglasses, the enormous green neon hat, undeniable energy, and the sassiest lyrics a young girl had sung in the top forty ever:

2 inches or a yard rock hard or if it's saggin'
I ain't 2 proud 2 beg (no).

Who the hell was TLC? And who was that little rapper with the dirty mouth and the condom over her eye? She looked fucking crazy.

Oooooooohhh...On the TLC Tip would eventually sell 6 million records. Not a bad opening statement for the group of three young, female artists from Atlanta's burgeoning hip-hop scene. Left Eye rapped and sang, and she had her hands all over the album art and video concepts. She designed the stage sets, dressed the band, and was in large part responsible for the group's image; an image that would help push them over the top and into American living rooms via MTV and late-night-television appearances.

At a time when mainstream hip-hop fashion was becoming predictable—gold chains, red, black, and green African flag color schemes, matching stage outfits—Lisa Lopes added bombastic colors, originality, and social consciousness to her look.

One day while getting dressed, she took note of the condom and the safety pin on her dresser. HIV was on the rise; a scary time to be a sexually active young adult. Not talking about it wasn't doing anyone any good, so why accept the fact that carrying a condom for a young woman was anything *but* responsible? Why rely on a guy to protect you when you could do it yourself? And why hide the fact? Rather than throwing the condom and the safety pin in her purse before heading out, she pinned them to her pants. And that simple, couldn't-give-a-shit subversive fashion statement by one of America's rising young stars was a glaring message that it was okay to talk about safe sex publicly. It was an answer to Salt-N-Pepa's "Let's Talk About Sex" single from two years earlier. A chorus of young, empowered, female, musical voices was helping shape the national conversation around HIV and Lisa "Left Eye" Lopes was adding hers, and because she was who she was, she was making the conversation *fun*.

At least that was how some took it. Others just saw it as some crazy, famous chick with condoms pinned to her clothes, which, given Lisa's behavior at the time, wasn't so hard to believe. As her success increased, so did her drinking. Alter Ego Nikki was bum-rushing the show, and Lisa wasn't afraid to cast blame. After whatever crazy behavior would land her in trouble, Lisa would claim, "That ain't me. That's Nikki. My evil twin, who came from within, whom I blame for all of my sins."

Getting up on the bar at the club and dancing?

Mugging for the camera with a condom over her eye?

Being a relentless flirt when it suited her?

According to Lisa, that was all Nikki.

Sometimes Nikki and Lisa joined forces, like on the night when TLC won two Grammys, and she called out her record label for overcharging them on production. From the press podium after the show, Lisa claimed that the group was broke and insinuated that it was due to her greedy label and producers. Not exactly the message the music industry wants to hear after it coronates a young group of stars.

Management and LaFace responded by telling the press that the trash talk was all just part of a power play: the group were simply trying to force them into a new contract. TLC eventually filed for bankruptcy, a filing which was upheld, and the group did indeed win a new contract, settling out of court. Nikki wasn't all bad.

Lisa's outspokenness and occasional drunken visits from Nikki were only part of the problem. Lisa's new boyfriend, Atlanta Falcons wide receiver Andre Rison, was no good, either.

Lisa was crazy for Andre, and Andre was crazy for Lisa. He liked the idea of having a famous girlfriend, so the two quickly moved in together. But despite her desire for a stable, monogamous relationship, Andre could not be tied down to one woman. He was unfaithful, jealous, possessive, short-tempered, violent, and, when not on the football field, almost always drunk and belligerent.

One night, outside an Atlanta nightclub, Lisa refused to pick up whatever bullshit Andre was putting down, and the argument became physical, escalating to the point of shots being fired off by Andre in an effort to gain control of both the situation and his girlfriend.

Cops were on the scene quickly and tensions defused, but Lisa refused to press charges. She loved the big thug. Number 80 was a handful, but she'd break him. She had so much faith in Andre that she had his digits tattooed on her left biceps.

The lyrics for TLC's smash single "Creep" seemed to have spun out of Lisa and Andre's tumultuous, unfaithful relationship. The message was clear: Cheat on me and I'll give it right back. But Lisa hated the song. Mainly the sentiment. She believed in fidelity to her core. Despite the outrageous clothes, fiery attitude, and over-the-top behavior, Lisa "Left Eye" Lopes from TLC was traditional in one regard: She was a one-man woman. Crazy.

Everybody thought they knew Lisa Lopes. But most didn't. They knew Nikki. Nikki was who'd come around after the drinks started flowing. Nikki was who'd bring the party to the next level. Hell, Nikki was a party unto herself, and she didn't take shit from anyone. Kinda like a scrappy little pit bull. She was cute but had a lot of bite in her.

Lisa, on the other hand, hung back. Quiet for the most part. Head in the clouds. Wondering about this. Ready to get into that. She had poems. Dance moves. Outfits she was designing. Beats on the brain.

Left Eye burning down the house by way of her shitty boyfriend's new sneaker stash.

Movies she was going to one day star in. TV shows she planned on hosting. A documentary in Honduras she wanted to shoot.

Together, Nikki and Lisa were unstoppable. One was filled with a careless electric feel and the other with boundless creativity.

But they hated each other. Lisa knew her creativity would eventually overpower Nikki's drunken bullshit one way or another. Then Nikki wouldn't be showing up at any more parties. And with Nikki gone, it'd just be Lisa and Andre. Alone at last.

And that was what happened.

Lisa got it together. Put all her shit in one bag, so to speak, and moved into Andre's big-ass house over in Alpharetta, cut back on the drinking, not entirely but just enough to keep Nikki at bay. She thought that mellowing out and moving in with Andre would bring calm to the hectic life that comes with being a major pop artist dating an NFL star. But Andre Rison's demons ran deep, and as best she tried, Lisa was no match for Andre's jealous, narcissistic ways or his roving eye.

The man could not keep his dick in his pants.

Out all night.

Every night.

Full of shit.

All the time.

After catching him in bed in the guest room with that slut from Velvet or the Cheetah or wherever Andre happened to be partying that night, Lisa knew she'd taken this as far as she could on her own.

There was no way to break this dude. And she loved him, so breaking him was the only option. But Lisa didn't give up easy. So the decision was made. She needed Nikki. Nikki was a crazy, drunk fool, but that type of crazy earned respect from men like Andre.

So on the night of June 9, 1994, Lisa decided that the party was on. She got dressed *up* and headed downtown. If Andre was going to go out all night every night and openly cheat on her, then Lisa "Left Eye" Lopes of TLC was going to go out and get hers. Let him experience what it's like to wait up all night for someone to come home.

Stay out all night. Come back wearing that dress that drives him wild, the short one, with the slit that runs high up the side and show him exactly what he's been missing.

Five a.m. She figured that was late enough. Even if Andre went out himself, he'd be home by then with ample time to stew over where she was. So when Lisa pulled in Andre's driveway just after five in the morning and realized Andre wasn't even home yet? Nikki went through the fucking roof. Nuh-uh. That *prick*. And just as that thought hit her lips, Andre's Benz pulled in the driveway behind her.

Oh boy.

Andre got out of the car. Saw what Lisa was wearing and that she herself was just getting home, and freaked the fuck out. Who did this woman think she was dressing like that and staying out all night?

Nuh-uh. Nikki...*Lisa* smacked Andre in the face. Fuck this guy. Who did he think *he* was?

From there the fight moved into the house. Both of them drunk and screaming nonsense at the top of their lungs. Taking turns throwing random shit at each other until it came to blows. Andre wasn't a small man, either. Lisa...was a very small woman. The blow to the face came and went. Lisa didn't know when or how. Nikki was in control now. Typical.

Once the fight died down, Lisa went in to the bathroom to clean up. She took a glimpse in the mirror but didn't recognize her own face. Badly bruised. She became enraged.

You know what you gotta do, right? Nikki pushed the issue.

Kill the prick.

Lisa stormed out of the bathroom intent on doing just that but thought better of it and took a beat. She retreated to the walk in closet off of her bedroom to get some headspace and calm down.

That was when she saw the shoes. Hundreds of them. Brand-new, sparkling white tennis shoes. All of them size 12 and mens. That selfish prick! All mens! Nikki wanted to know where Lisa's shoes were. *Oh yeah, THAT ASSHOLE DIDN'T BUY YOU ANY! He bought himself a new identical pair for every goddamn day of the year but he didn't buy you jack shit!*

Shut up, Nikki.

Fuck you, Lisa.

Lisa grabbed the shoes and headed back into the bathroom. She threw them in the tub. Hit the closet again and went to grab lighter fluid and some matches. Back to the bathroom. Past the stranger in the mirror again. She doused the shoes with lighter fluid and then:

Lit a match.

The fire went up quick. It immediately started spreading. How? Lisa had no idea. At first she froze in fear. Then? She moved. And the next thing she knew, she was watching her boyfriend's house burn down on the six o'clock morning news.

Just. Like. That.

She didn't mean to do it. Really. But he deserved it.

Crazy.

The news coverage the next day was ridiculous. Almost entirely one-sided. Against Lisa! Sure, she burned her boyfriend's mansion down *but it was because he beat the piss out of her.* And let's not forget *the dude was a professional football player.*

The guy who openly cheated on her, controlled her, abused her. The guy whose fist imprint could practically still be seen on the massive bruise on Lisa's face in her mugshot from that day. *That guy* was the victim?

Yes. A mug shot. Lisa had turned herself in and eventually

The talented and fiery Lisa "Left Eye" Lopes.

pleaded guilty, and she was sentenced to five months probation and locked up in a halfway house for a month. Andre Rison played football and quite likely kept banging strippers on his nights off.

Lisa voluntarily went to rehab, and with a clear head wrote the smash TLC hit, "Waterfalls," which was included on the album *CrazySexyCool*, released later in the fall of 1994. The song helped propel the album to 23 million in record sales.

But the success wouldn't last. Lisa eventually fell out with T-Boz and Chilli.

The fire, the rehab, and the elevated success achieved largely through Lisa's writing of a smash hit changed things for the young star. She now knew what she alone was capable of, with a clear head anyway.

Creatively, "Waterfalls" made her—in her mind at least—a proven commodity, so she herself was a safe bet. The only bet. Relying on the influence of others was only fucking up Lisa's plans. And Lisa, after rehab, was hell-bent on not being held back…by anyone. No more TLC. No more Nikki. Lisa Lopes had arrived. She wanted it her way. Or nothing at all.

Lisa went on to sign with Suge Knight's Death Row Records and began talks with David Bowie—of all people—about a collaboration. Now that was *really* crazy.

She had recorded a number of tracks for a subsidiary of Death Row Records called Tha Row, and the album, fittingly, was going to be titled, *N.I.N.A.*, which stood for "new identity not applicable." Then Lisa headed to Honduras for a retreat. She had this clear-headed vibe on lock. But the trip wasn't going as planned. Lisa started picking up bad feelings. Having premonitions that an evil spirit was haunting her, that death was on the creep.

One night, she and her assistant hopped in their car to go for a ride. The heavy, humid Honduran air was stifling and a drive would do them good, or so they thought. Once in the car, the bad feeling started up again. As they zipped down the winding road from their village, they passed a dead horse on the roadside. In unison, a flock of birds up above let out a screeching death rattle as it moved from one tree to another. And then a blunt thud against their moving car.

They immediately pulled over. On the road at their feet in front of their SUV was a critically injured ten-year-old boy. Quickly, they pulled him into the car and raced off to the nearest hospital, Lisa held him the whole way. His blood stuck to her sweaty skin in the sweltering central American night air. The boy died at the hospital. Lisa paid his medical and eventual funeral bills and later compensated the family for their loss.

Her guilt was immense. Lisa couldn't shake the feeling that the accident was supposed to take her life, not the boy's.

She was convinced that the same evil spirit was following her.

April 25, 2002. A few weeks after the accident, Lisa Lopes changed out of the outfit she was wearing that day. It was all white. She then chose an outfit of all black. Got dressed without a destination in mind and decided a ride was needed to get some headspace.

Lisa's SUV zipped by the village again and past the dead horse, now just a loosely assembled pile of bones being picked over by a few vultures. Vultures. Death. More signs. The SUV sped away trying to outrun Lisa's demons.

She was distracted. Moving way too fast, head in the clouds. Wondering about this. Ready to get into that. The guilt was an aching pit in her stomach. Part of her thought she would never recover. How could she write or perform again, with this feeling rolling around in her gut, with death chasing her down? The car accelerated. The breeze felt good on her skin. And then, her SUV's rear end seemed to get out ahead of itself. The SUV swerved. To the left. Then to the right. At the speed it was going there was no recovering. The SUV then flew violently off the side of the road, into the air, and then down into the ditch. The vehicle was totaled. Lisa Lopes died on the scene almost immediately.

At the age of thirty. With a clear head and a wide-open future creeping around the corner. Lisa "Left Eye" Lopes had left crazy behind when she shed herself of Nikki. She was about to move onto her second act, creatively. Lisa had gotten her way. And now? After speeding away from her demons in a fast moving SUV? It was over. There was nothing.

Her casket was engraved with what might have been the most poignant lines she ever rapped: "Dreams are hopeless aspirations in hopes of coming true / Believe in yourself / The rest is up to me and you."

CHAPTER 10

PHIL SPECTOR

PHIL SPECTOR'S NASALLY VOICE sang through the crackle of the Pac Bell telephone line. On the other end, sixteen-year-old Annette Kleinbard, the singer in his group the Teddy Bears, was unimpressed. But Phil was undeterred. He hung up and beat a hasty retreat to his bedroom at 726 North Hayworth in Los Angeles's Fairfax neighborhood, slammed the door shut so his overbearing mom would get the picture and leave him alone. He proceeded to bat the song's chords around the neck of his Gibson acoustic guitar while the melody to the song he was trying to finish writing banged around in his brain. Finally, exhausted and having made little progress, he passed out on his fully made bed, completely clothed, guitar at his side.

The dream was intense.

It's raining. Hard like it always is in the dream. And it's Phil at his dad's grave. It's the funeral all over again but it isn't 1949, it's present day, 1958, and Phil is no longer a nine-year-old. He's eighteen. As he is in real life, but unlike in real life, in his dream Phil is already a success. He's dressed for the part of an earth-shaking music man. His style is part hepcat, part greaser. The funeral guests all know who he is, but he can't make out their faces.

Some approach him, but Phil's bodyguards—yes, bodyguards—keep them away.

He's staring at his father's headstone. His mother is seated next to him. She leans over and whispers to him that she will never forgive Phil for what his father did—sucked on the end of a carbon monoxide–filled hose until the lights went out in the Bronx. The words stung. So did the grief. It overwhelmed him at times. The grief put him on an emotional wave of extremes: one moment higher than the Hollywood hills, and the next lower than the rats that scurried shamefully over the New York City street corners he spent his early childhood on. Phil held focus on the headstone and concentrated. He tried hard to make out the inscription;

TO KNOW HIM WAS TO LOVE HIM.

Phil shot up, awake, in his bed. Sweat covering his body. So much sweat that he thought for a second he'd pissed himself. No matter. He grabbed his guitar and strummed the chords to the song he was trying to impress Annette with:

Open D major. Then the trusty A7. He walked his finger up to the B minor chord, picking out the bass notes in the process. Then to the G.

Again.

And then he started singing the same line he'd sang to Annette over the phone but substituted the word *was* with *is*, shifting the tense from the past to the present and thus completely altering the song's sentiment. It was no longer a mixed-up kid's dark lament of a dead parent, it was relatable teenage heartache.

"To Know Him *Is* to Love Him," well, that's saying something. We all knew *him*, Phil thought. Or at least the girls at Fairfax High knew him. He was the guy in the hall with the letter jacket and the big smile. Kinda boring. Totally sweet. Always there when you needed him.

Phil filled in some lines over the chord progression:

To know, know, know him is to love, love, love him
Just to see him smile, makes my life worthwhile.

The chorus wasn't for Phil or his dad. It was for them, those girls. It was all they were going to focus on, anyway.

He knew what those kids wanted: He had been studying them from the outside, looking in. Ever since his mother uprooted young Phil and his elder sister, Shirley, from the Bronx to California, he hadn't fit in. You can take the boy out of the Bronx, but you can't take the Bronx out of the boy, especially the Bronx accent, which in Phil's case was filtered through an especially nasally voice. It's never easy being the new kid, but when you're the new kid, and your voice is the type that whatever bully coined the term *pipsqueak* had in mind, then it's especially difficult. So Phil didn't contribute. Didn't speak up all that often. Instead, he observed, like any great writer. But Phil's time to share his observations with his peers eventually came, and he shared through song. He would let teenage America have that chorus to themselves. It was his gift.

The verses on the other hand. They were all his:

Everyone says there'll come a day when I'll walk alongside of him
Yes, just to know him is to love him.

Phil was speaking to his dad. It was his way of not letting his dad leave. For everyone else it was a pop song. And it was perfect for its day, sentimental like the Pat Boone and Perry Como hits that reached back to the postwar cultural safety net that parents could easily fall into but imbued with the rock 'n' roll backseat teenage yearning of the Everly Brothers and Ricky Nelson that made kids want to jump out of their PF Flyers. Phil, still just a kid himself, focused on the yearning part. More specifically, he focused on his lust as he lip-synced the song's lyrics and avoided eye contact with the buxomy blond dancers swaying in the audience in front of him on Dick Clark's *American Bandstand.*

Phil on guitar, beside Annette singing, was a boy brimming with lust. Since the release of "To Know Him Is to Love Him" and its chart-climbing success, the world had opened up to Phil. He sang the backups, eagerly anticipating the postshow party where he'd get up close and personal with the *Bandstand* dancers despite the fact that physically, he was a far cry from the Troy Donahue type he'd written about in his No. 1 single. Yes, No. 1. Suicidal grief masquerading as unrequited teenage love rocketed Phil Spector's Teddy Bears to the top of the charts, but he still cut a diminutive figure on top of the bandstand. Five foot five, barely taller than Annette, and a square-looking haircut that wanted to be a rock 'n' roll pompadour but instead looked like a boyish flattop, largely because of his rapidly thinning hair. He was more nerd without a fashion sense than rebel without a cause. And his outfit, more Canter's busboy than James Dean; a lame boxy-white blazer that Phil clearly had trouble filling out, along with a flattened Western-style bow tie. Hardly the television debut of the next Elvis Presley, whose physical presence and prowess was so impressive that Phil was compelled to take the name of his group from Elvis's recent hit "Teddy Bear" despite the fact that Elvis—unlike Phil—couldn't write his own songs.

But Phil Spector *could* write his own songs. And he'd write lots after "To Know Him Is to Love Him." Many of them would become the most culturally consequential pop songs in history and would make Phil Spector more money than he'd ever be able to spend in one lifetime. He would become a millionaire by the time he was twenty-two. And because he had made all of this money himself, he reasoned that *doing* everything himself was the move. Writing the songs wasn't enough; he had to produce them as well. And since he couldn't trust the songs he had written and produced to any old record label, he started his own company, Philles Records, after cutting his teeth as a staff producer at Dune Records. He started the label with fellow producer Lester Sill, but Phil would buy out Sill within a year. Partners were dead notes. Phil would rather bet on himself, play the open chords.

Phil was shouting over the sound of the jet's turbo compressors and completely ignoring the flight's stewardess. He was trying to make a point to his favorite Beatle. "Look, John, baby, you're gonna be all right. We don't *all* carry guns, okay? Besides, Kennedy couldn't keep his little Irish schmeckel in his pants and everyone knew it, okay? You brought your wife and your baby with you. You're gonna be fine. As long as Paul learns all the words to 'The Yellow Rose of Texas.'"

Phil kept fast-talking John, denying him a chance to laugh at the joke.

"I'm just teasing you, Johnny baby. Don't look at me like that. I'm telling you, you're gonna be fine in the States. And you're gonna be safe. Just keep *your* little schmeckel in Cynthia's purse."

"Who said anything about it being little, Phil?" John deadpanned.

Phil Spector, the so-called "first tycoon of teen" roared over the sounds of the Boeing 707 en route from London's Heathrow airport to the recently named John F. Kennedy International Airport in New York City on February 7, 1964.

He stopped and spoke to John as he paced up and down the

aisles. The Beatles would later dub Phil "the man who walked to America" because he paced so much on that plane ride.

Ringo was giddy. Grab-assing with the stewardesses. George was quiet. Up front talking to the pilot. Paul was in all seriousness trying to learn "The Yellow Rose of Texas" on John's acoustic, and John, per usual, was tense. Phil's pacing probably didn't help. The Beatles' skyrocketing success in the States on the heels of Kennedy's assassination had him worried about his band's first trip to the United States.

So it was left to Phil Spector, the producer and songwriter of the Ronettes' "Be My Baby," the earth-shattering smash hit that rattled the creative cages of the most successful musicians on both sides of the pond, to convince John Lennon—one-quarter of arguably the most popular group on the planet—to cool out and get ready to enjoy himself in America. If nothing else, Phil's own nervous energy served as a barometer for John. At least he wasn't as high-strung as Phil.

John was listening, though. He respected Phil. Phil was smart. His talent was immense and obvious.

It's no stretch to say that Phil Spector was a genius. One of those rare talents that created something completely new, almost out of thin air. Phil Spector's recording style was something that had never been heard before in popular music, or anywhere else for that matter. It was a "wall of sound," and Phil held the patent. Drawing on the massive lush orchestral sounds of classical music and funneled through the reality of having to record in tight studio confines, the result was a dense and layered sound that was exhilarating coming out of the tiny jukebox and car stereo speakers of the day.

Phil took it one step further and invented "groups" out of thin air to suit the sounds he was creating. Normally, to that point any-way, a professional songwriter would write a song. Then the song's publisher, the record label, the hired producer, and to some extent the songwriter would find a singer or a group that was either a known commodity with an audience or a new star on the come-up whose future they were investing in. That song would then be given to the singer to record with the producer and eventually released through the record label.

What Phil did was cut *everyone* out of the equation. He was the first producer of note to also write the songs. And he would not be slowed or deterred by the complications of finding or working with existing stars. To Phil Spector, making music, *making hits,* wasn't necessarily about the singer or the song. It was about the producer. The man who could pull the track together and craft it into a hit by any means necessary. When a singer or a group couldn't be found in short order, Phil would just invent one. Literally. Out of thin air. *We have this great song I wrote but no group to record it? Doesn't matter— pull some backing singers in from the session down the hall, slap a name on them, something like "Bob B. Soxx and the Blue Jeans," get the song on tape, then wax, then ship it, get it played on radio, and voila—a top-ten hit. Oh, there's another song, "He's a Rebel," being recorded over at Liberty Records and it's got real potential but someone else wrote it? The demo sounds* perfect *for the Crystals, the girl group I've been riding up the charts with lately. The Crystals* need *to record it before Liberty makes it a hit first. Oh the Crystals are in LA and can't get to NYC anytime soon for the session? Just as well. The song is a beast. The melody likely isn't one the Crystals will be able to handle in the studio anyway. Okay, no sweat. I'll get my girl, Darlene Love, and her group, the Blossoms, to record it on the quick. Darlene is in town and she can sing anything. Fuck Liberty. We'll get it released before them. And you know what? Forget about the Blossoms. They're not rocketing out of my stable of stars as quickly as the Crystals, so even though the Blossoms recorded the tune, let's credit it to the Crystals because they're more popular and have a better chance at success and because I'm the producer and I know what's best and voila—a No. 1 hit.*

It's hard to argue with success. Phil's unconventional approach to talent and recording made him the most successful pop music producer on the planet. Between 1961 and 1966 he charted more than twenty top-forty hits with acts like the aforementioned Crystals, the Righteous Brothers, and the Ronettes.

The Ronettes, for Phil, were his greatest creation, and their smash hit "Be My Baby" *made him* in the eyes of many of his contemporaries. Not only was it a hit upon its release in 1963, its sound was groundbreaking. If ever there was a recording to define the "wall of sound," it was "Be My Baby." The recording relied on a mass of instrumentation: the biggest of beats with multiple guitars, pianos, and horns all layered on top of one another, and Phil's favorite new young female singer, Ronnie Spector, sailing over the top of it all with her sultry vocals.

The song hit No. 2 on the Billboard Hot 100 and was unavoidable in 1963. The Beatles were obsessed. As were the Rolling Stones, whom Phil and the Ronettes had just wrapped up a headlining tour with—the Stones opening for them—back in the UK. Phil, with his knack for being in the right place at the right time, found his way onto the Beatles' first flight to America, Pan Am 101, and did his best to convince his new friend John that not all Americans were gun-crazed lunatics.

But Phil was himself a gun-crazed American. A couple years earlier, back in Philly after the *Bandstand* taping, Phil hit a public bathroom in the bus terminal. He was still in his stage duds looking very much out of place while relieving himself into one of those long, low, trough-like public urinals. From behind him, four street toughs bellowed out insults.

"Nice jacket," Tough No. 1 muttered.

"What are you, some type of Cowboy Shrimp?" Tough No. 2 asked. The rest laughed.

Phil, still facing the urinal, his penis in hand, turned his head over his right shoulder to assess just how deep the shit that he was about to be in was.

"Got something to say, Cowboy Shrimp?"

Phil said nothing. Just turned his head back to the wall. His urine reversed its course back up into his bladder. Phil was frozen with fear.

"I'm talking to you, Cowboy Shrimp. Don't ignore me!"

Phil kept quiet and tried to casually zip himself up. When he was done he turned around, kept his head down, and tried to briskly walk by them. Tough No. 1 threw his beefy shoulder into Phil, nearly knocking him off his feet and into Tough No. 2.

Tough No. 2: "You trying to start something, Cowboy Shrimp?"

Phil's eyes darted toward the exit door. He made a hasty break for it but it was no use. The four toughs were on him immediately. They threw him to the ground and laid a beating on him he'd never forget. Phil's anger at the situation was so intense he was nearly immune to the physical pain of the beating: the aching ribs from their kicks, the splintering headache from the round of punches his head endured. He made the decision right then and there: Never again would he go anywhere without protection.

They called it a "Peacemaker" but Phil never knew why. It was a violent instrument, the .45 Colt, a single-action revolver originally designed for standard military service back in the nineteenth century. The Peacemaker would come to be known as the "gun that won the West," but to Phil Spector, it just looked cool. Like something the Lone Ranger would use. It was Phil's first gun. He took it with him everywhere.

He gave John a look. "Hey, John, get a load of this." Phil, now in the seat on the Boeing next to John, hunched over and reached into his carry-on, pulling up by the walnut grip his fully loaded, blued .45 Colt. He kept himself hunched over with his hand still holding the gun in the bag, just high enough to give his favorite Beatle a real glimpse at his added security.

"Fuck, Phil. See, all you Americans are crazy."

"Nah, just careful."

John slid easily into his well-rehearsed John Wayne impersonation and replied back to Phil in his deepest Duke baritone, "Now you put that away before little Ringo sees it and gets even more excited."

Phil put the gun back into his bag and got up to pace again, but it wouldn't be the last time Phil would flash his steel to a musician.

Leonard Cohen, Dee Dee Ramone, and once again John Lennon would all—in later years—claim that Spector pulled his gun on them. But their stories were child's play compared to the tales of horror later told by the women in Phil Spector's life.

"Listen to that! The Righteous Brothers!!! 'You Lost That Lovin' Feelin'.' Hear that? Hear that voice? Listen to how big it is. Listen to how up front it is in the mix. Wait for it...Wait! There. The strings in the back. They're there but they don't take away from Bill's voice. You know why? Because Bill could lay it on. THICK. And because Bobby wasn't piping along with him and stepping on the vocal. Bobby was the sidecar. Bill was the tumbler. Rollin' and tumblin', baby. Listen to his voice effortlessly roll over the mix. Not even that orchestral percussion could step on it. Bill Medley had it. I had to sideline Bobby Hatfield. Bobby never forgave me. The song made him very rich, but still I'm the bad guy. What did

Phil Spector showing John Lennon his gun, on the Beatles' first flight to America.

he care, anyway? I made him more money with that song than he'd ever make in his life, and you know why? Because it didn't need a tenor. It wasn't a duet. It needed that big baritone that Bill had and that Bobby didn't. That deep, lonesome voice that sounds like it's whispering to you on a long, quiet drive; that is anchored by deep, swirling, emotional turmoil that the orchestra behind it is stewing up. IT WASN'T A FUCKING DUET, BOBBY! I'M SORRY! Now take your check and go to the bank!".

Phil Spector was on a rant. His little voice echoed through the vast corridors of his 8,600-square-foot residence, a dwelling with the appointed name of the Pyrenees Castle, overlooking the working-class town of Alhambra, California, like a monster in waiting. The sixty-nine-year-old producer was roaming through the enormous dwelling, alone save for servants tucked away for the night. Phil was keeping company with the dead, talking aloud to the ghost of his old friend, John Lennon. He knew Lennon was there with him as he spoke glowingly about their mutual childhood obsession, the King.

"Elvis's version wasn't bad but it wasn't as good, either. Elvis had that voice, too, John. You knew it. Well, I'm telling you, I KNOW it! Such a voice. He was a great singer. You have no idea how great he really was. I can't tell you *why* he was so great, but he was. He was sensational. He could do anything with that voice. I would have loved to have recorded him but the Colonel never would have allowed it. You know, ask some people who knew him, they'll tell you, when Elvis went in a room with Colonel Parker he was one way, when he came out he was another. The Colonel hypnotized him. That's the truth, too, I can tell you six or seven people who believe it who are not jive-ass people. I mean, he actually *changed*. You'd talk to Elvis and he'd be, 'Yes, yes, yes!' and then he'd go into that room with the Colonel and when he'd come out he'd be all, 'No, no, no.' Now, nobody can con you like that.

"Except the press, John. When the institutions line up against you, they can finish you. The LA County District Attorney's office; they haven't convicted anyone since Manson. Not O.J. Not Robert Blake. They're gunning for me. You know what I'm talking about, right? Because you had it worse off. You had Nixon coming at you. Pissed off that he wasn't a Kennedy and pissed off that you weren't an American. Cons. All of them. Nixon, the Kennedys, the institutions, the authorities, and the press. Especially the press! They're conning the public now. Telling 'em I killed that girl. Bullshit!"

Spittle was gathering at the corners of Phil's mouth. He sipped his crème de menthe from a chalice and sat down at the white piano, an exact replica of the one he'd recorded John's "Imagine" on. He plunked a few notes randomly and softly mumbled out a few words from "You've Lost That Lovin' Feelin'":

It makes me just feel like cryin'
Cause baby, something beautiful's dying.

The emotion of the lyrics was too much. He stood up and began pacing again to collect himself, turning his attention again to John.

"John, let me show you something. Look at my hands. I'm an old man. I couldn't have done it. That girl. Special? No, she wasn't special. There are thousands like her in LA. She could have been anybody. She *was* anybody. And what a mouth on her. She was drunk and loud and yeah, she wanted a ride home. Brought a bottle of tequila along with her. Then she wants to see the castle. It'd been a long night, but what do I do? I say, 'Yeah, come see the castle,' sure. And I thought I could score a piece of ass like I hadn't in a while, not that I didn't have opportunities."

Phil fell into the plush of one of his many armchairs. Sat and sunk his small, slippered feet into the shag of the burgundy carpet. He poured out more of the syrupy green liqueur, picked up a framed photograph of Lennon, and raised his chalice to toast him.

"To you, my friend." He sipped and breathed out slowly, loosening the stiffness in his neck.

"You want the truth, John? We get here, me and this girl, and I think, 'Let's take things to the next level, baby.' Did we? Wouldn't you like to know, John, you horny fuck. Maybe we did, maybe we didn't. I'll leave it at that. Anyway, then she's checking out all of my stuff. My records. My carousel horse. My Lawrence of Arabia digs. Wandering around from room to room. Maybe she gets into my gun room? Maybe she reaches into her purse? All I know is suddenly she's blown her fucking head off, right in my house. BOOM! In my castle. Right in that chair. She had no fucking right."

Phil's head felt light. He set the photo down where he could see it and placed his fingers at his temples, resting his elbows on the desk. The chair where it happened, a Louis XIV pushed up against the mirrored wall, had been replaced with a new one, covered in ivory damask. Clean. Like nothing happened.

Phil continued. He couldn't help himself. John was a captive audience. "Blood? Sure, there was blood, John. You of all people know about blood. And so I get a little woozy over seeing her like that and go outside and call to my driver. THEY say I said, 'I think I just killed somebody.' C'mon…

"'What, boss?' My driver wants to know. I tell him, 'I think I HAVE TO CALL somebody.' Which I have to repeat three fucking times. Good guy, Adriano, but pretty much zero *Inglés*. So I yell, 'I think I have to CALL SOMEBODY!' And I go back inside, close the door, draw the drapes. I put some records on and wait. It's maybe four, five in the morning. The sky is getting light when the cops get here. They're waiting out there for a while and who the fuck knows why? Did they think they'd intimidate me? And then,

BAM, they're in here and they throw me to the ground, John. They break my septum. Would you look at my fucking septum? And I tell them I didn't kill this stupid bitch and they must think I'm resisting because they Taser the fuck out of me. I pass out. Look at me. I weigh 130 pounds. Do I look like someone who has to be Tasered, and by a dozen giant cops, no less?"

Phil paced about, patted his hand against his wig, a mod cut, combed forward, the color of a new penny.

"Marta? *Estas en la cocina? Mi amor? Por favor, tráeme otra botella,* for fuck's sake. I know you love me, baby. Everybody loves me. They want to be me but they lack courage. I can be anything I want. A fucking UN translator. Marta, *dónde estás?* I know Spanish. I love the Latin beat. I understand the Latin beat. Where the fuck is Marta?"

Phil shuffled over to the piano. Sat down. Exhausted. Distracted. He rubbed the two cigarette burns that he'd imagined Lennon had made with a pair of forgotten Gitanes. Removed his wire-framed, lavender-tinted glasses. Pinched the bridge of his nose. Looked down at the keys, a row of perfect pearly ivory. Teeth. Her top front teeth had been blown clear out of her head. Her face caved in. Phil caved into himself with shame.

"Let me ask you something, John? Why would I shoot her? Why would I, Philip Harvey Spector, shoot that girl? I had no motive. I...Had...No...Motive.

"Even your guy had a motive. That fat Chapman fuck. He thought you were a sellout, and you know what? He was right! And Kennedy's guys, they had motive, too. But me? No motive. *Sin motivo!*"

But Phil Spector did have a motive. Fear. Fear of being left alone. Everyone he loved, it seemed, eventually left him.

First, his good friend Lenny Bruce left him. Dead. Overdosed at forty.

Ronnie Spector driving around town with a dummy version of her jealous, possessive, psychotic husband, Phil.

Then there was Ronnie. That one hurt really bad. He fell in love with her while her star was in ascent. She was just in high school when Phil produced her singing "Be My Baby." Phil didn't need convincing. He was ready and willing to accept the invitation of the song's title. That voice: unabashed New York City, baby. And those hips. Ronnie was perfect for Phil, but there was the problem of one Mrs. Annette Spector, Phil's wife, a singer whom he had also produced in a group called the Spectors Three, which were basically a way less successful version of the Teddy Bears. But Ronnie wasn't Annette. Ronnie was special. And worth the headache of busting up his marriage for. Phil threw himself into making Ronnie a star. He took her nickname, "Ronnie," and turned it into a group name: the Ronettes. He threw her sister and her cousin up onstage next to her so it actually looked like a group. Voila. Write a hit. Record the hit. Release the hit. Again, voila. Star. Next? Marry her so she can't up and leave you. So that's what Phil did. He and Ronnie hitched up in 1968, the year after he had divorced Annette. Phil was quick to assert control in his second marriage, just like in the recording studio. The next year, the couple adopted a son—which Phil insisted Ronnie pretend she had given birth to. In Phil's estimation, it was more of a sign of success to be biological parents, so they sent out birth announcements, inferring that Ronnie had given birth. Unlike Phil's controlling nature in the studio, his controlling nature in the marriage did not yield successful results. Phil kept Ronnie locked up in their mansion for months at a time, refusing to let her out of his sight. When he did allow her to leave—for a maximum of twenty minutes at a time—he made her drive around with a life-sized dummy of Phil, complete with his signature cigarette hanging from his lips. Ronnie found an escape via alcohol, but where most habitual alcohol abuse can be a false escape, for Ronnie it was real: Phil put her in a sanitarium after every time she got drunk, which to her was a newfound freedom. She would drink to the depths of drunkenness every other month just to gain extended stays outside of the mansion. One time when Phil came to the sanitarium to collect Ronnie, she told him she wanted a divorce. He persuaded her to reconsider with a surprise gift: a pair of six-year-old twin boys he had adopted. No way was she going to leave him after that kind of pressure, he figured. Just six months later, when Ronnie could no longer take the psychological torture, she escaped barefoot and broke with her mother, under the ruse of "going for a walk" after Phil had shown her mom the coffin he kept in his basement. The one he said her daughter would end up in if she ever tried leaving.

And then there was John Lennon. He left Phil too. But that was different. A gun-crazed lunatic took him away, despite Phil's early assurances to the contrary.

And those weren't the only ones who tried leaving Phil Spector. Phil thought about them all, sitting in court on trial for the murder of Lana Clarkson. They brought up Ronnie, sure, but now they were laying it on thick for the jury. Trotting out testimony after testimony from every other wide-eyed cocktail waitress and rock 'n' roll wannabe who'd crossed paths with Phil in the last twenty years.

First there was the photographer, Stephanie Jennings, who testi-fied that after the Rock and Roll Hall of Fame inductions in New York back in 1994, Phil, who had a suite down the hall from her at the Carlyle Hotel, rang her up in her room and asked her to join him. She refused. Phil insisted. She was adamant. A few minutes later, Phil was outside her room with a gun and a chair. He wedged the chair against her hotel room doorknob, effectively locking her in and repeatedly yelled to her, "You ain't going nowhere." Stephanie called 911 and the cops came. Phil talked his way out of it and the incident was squashed.

Then there was the cocktail waitress, Melissa Grosvenor, who went back to Phil's castle with him after a Beverly Hills dinner. When she later told him she wanted to go home, Phil pulled out his gun, held it hard against her temple, and said, "If you try to leave I'm going to kill you." She did as she was told and stayed put. The next morning she split. Never to return to Phil despite his constant phone calls. When she failed to call him back, Phil left a message telling her, "I've got machine guns and I know where you live."

Phil Spector was mad. A genius, yes, but mad. The prosecution said so as they deftly strung together a narrative depicting a brilliant mind who had a penchant for violence and a strong dislike for women who tried leaving him. The narrative culminated with the murder of Lana Clarkson, a talented B-movie actress turned cocktail waitress who'd gone home with Phil Spector one night. She died in Phil's foyer, with her leopard print purse on her shoulder, where she'd been sitting in his Louis XIV chair just moments before her death in the familiar position of someone waiting to leave. The jury wasn't entirely buying it. They weren't convinced one way or another. Phil's high-priced defense team succeeded in planting reasonable doubt in the minds of some of the jurors, resulting in a mistrial. But when he was tried again, Phil would be convicted. Nineteen years to life.

Behind bars, Phil kept company with his ghosts. Sometimes Lenny visited but mostly John. John was loyal like that.

"Look, John. I'm gonna tell you something. She kissed that fucking gun like she was in love with it. I have no idea why. How would I know? I'd only met her that night and I felt kind of sorry for her, but she had a sense of humor and I thought what the hell, John, we all gotta laugh, right?

"But was it worth it? Hell no. She died, John. AT MY HOUSE! She got blood everywhere. Blood on my favorite white coat. John, it was a fucking mess. Then it's four, five months for the coroner to decide it's a homicide? So they charge me. Then they send me to jail because this bitch blows herself away in my house?

"There was no case, John. I'm telling you. It was a suicide. Probably an accidental fucking suicide. Maybe an on-fucking-purpose suicide. But a goddamn suicide nonetheless.

"The jury, that first time. Couldn't come to a consensus. Deadlocked. Mistrial. Then the next jury comes back guilty. You know why? The press! Robert Fucking Blake. FUCKING O. J. SIMPSON, JOHN! They needed their celebrity conviction. Me. I'm him. That's who. Not some other guy. But really, that original jury had it on the first take. No one gets it on the first take. Not even you. Not even Elvis. But I gotta hand it to them. They got it. You know why? Because it wasn't a homicide. It was just some depressed washed-up actress, fucked up on Vicodin, drunk, swinging around a bottle of Cuervo, who somehow gets my gun. A gun that turns out to be from Texas. I don't know how, John, okay? Look, she kissed the gun. She was making a kind of joke about it, like she was giving it fucking head or something and she accidentally fired it. There's no way I could have fired that gun. Look at that. Look at my hands shake! I can't even hold my fucking dick, let alone a gun. I wouldn't have put the gun in her mouth. I didn't want her gone, John.

"I wanted her to stay. I never want them to leave. But they all leave! All of them. Lenny, you, Ronnie…all of them. My old man, even. That hump couldn't stick around at least until I was out of short pants? No, he has to suck down on a gas hose. The pain is so bad? Being a father? Being a husband? Being a man? He can't take it so he takes it out on the arches and just up and leaves. Kills himself. John…John? Where did you go, don't leave, John. Come back. JOHN. Listen. The guards let me have this little record player. I've got some Elvis records we can listen to. John…John! Don't leave!"

CHAPTER 11

SKINNY ELVIS

ELVIS PRESLEY DIDN'T TAKE DRUGS for recreation. He took drugs for physical self-governance. Elvis didn't smoke grass, and despite what the interior decoration of the Jungle Room might have suggested, Elvis didn't stay up late with the boys blasting rails of cocaine. Nor was Elvis on some spiritual quest to break down the walls of perception through hallucinatory exploration. He didn't take LSD or mushrooms or peyote. Elvis was just trying to get through his day.

Speed to keep up. Downers to come down. Crash. Wake. Repeat.

The more this pattern continued, the more Elvis introduced additional pills into the mix to try and maintain himself physically and mentally. And with more drugs came more side effects.

Ethinamate, methaqualone, codeine, barbiturates, meperidine, morphine, and Valium were all prescribed to Elvis, and all were in his system the day he died. Chronic use of larger-than-recommended doses of (and/or sudden withdrawal from) the regular use of ethinamate can lead to central nervous system complications that manifest through hallucinations, delusions, and disorientation. The overuse of methaqualone can lead to insomnia and delirium marked by vivid nightmares, paranoid delusions, extreme fear, and visual hallucinations. Serious side effects of codeine include mental disturbances and hallucinations. Barbiturates decrease rapid eye movement during sleep—when dreaming happens—so withdrawal from the drug can lead to sleep disruption, including but not limited to the following symptoms: nightmares, vivid dreaming, insomnia, and hallucination.

In short, Elvis couldn't sleep. Not even in the cozy, heavily curtained confines of his master bedroom at Graceland. He couldn't tell if it was the pills or his stomach. In all honesty, he had no idea which pills he'd taken or when. He'd taken so many that he gave up keeping track. Nor could he remember what he had eaten that day, or the previous night, that had his stomach in knots. It was probably the meatloaf. He ate it pretty much daily. Or maybe it was the BBQ pizza. Probably both. His stomach hardly ever felt this bad. He was in poor health. He knew it. But he also knew he'd whip himself back into shape on the next tour, which was scheduled to begin imminently. The Colonel had been eager for Elvis to embark on these dates to help start bringing in cash again and to, of course, help Elvis get back to the business of being Elvis Presley, an idyllic version of himself that he was completely incapable of living up to on the morning of August 16, 1977.

Right now he wasn't "Elvis Presley." He was Fat Elvis. A bloated mess of a man. He weighed nearly 350 pounds and was for the most part bedridden save for various trips to the Jungle Room or to his piano or for a couple minutes on his racquetball court where he'd swat weakly at volleys from various members of his entourage and stumble around until finally running out of breath. They'd let him win and he'd never forgive them for it.

Little did his entourage or anyone know that Elvis, at the time, was suffering from an enlarged heart, twice the size of what it should have been, and was presenting signs of advanced cardiovascular disease. The pills didn't help and neither did the diet of rich, cholesterol-filled Southern cooking he'd been eating his whole life. His bowel was twice the size it was supposed to be and had been housing an impacted stool for the past four months. But to Elvis, the thing that had him most fucked-up at the moment wasn't the pills or the upset stomach, it was what was on his mind.

That Streisand song would not stop rolling around in his head, "My Heart Belongs to Me." Elvis knew it well. Hell, everyone knew it well. It had been No. 1 on the charts for the better part of the summer of '77. But that was not how Elvis came to know the tune. The song was originally slated to be part of Barbra Streisand's Academy Award–winning movie *A Star Is Born*, released in December 1976. Elvis was made aware of it when Streisand pitched him to star opposite her as the film's male lead.

Elvis was hyped on it. He believed in Barbra and had ever since he saw her show back in '69 at the International Hotel in Vegas. She seemed taken by him. He vibed on her. He could tell she was more than just an eager-to-please starlet. So when she and her hair-dresser-boyfriend came to him with *A Star Is Born* six years later, he knew Barbra could deliver the goods. Plus, the role was perfect for him: A self-destructive singer-songwriter rock star dealing with his midlife demons as his star begins its descent? Sign me up, Elvis thought. Plus, Streisand was one of the biggest stars of the decade, and Elvis hadn't had a hit since "Burning Love," three years earlier. Elvis agreed to do the movie.

So the Colonel went to work negotiating for his boy.

He wanted top billing for Elvis, despite the fact that it was Barbra Streisand's project and that Streisand was arguably the bigger star at the time, having received an Oscar nomination for *The Way We Were* in '73, after sharing the 1968 Best Actress award (with Katharine Hepburn) for *Funny Girl*. Nevertheless, the Colonel went on to demand that all drug references be stripped from the script because they would be harmful to Elvis's image, despite the fact that drugs were the motivating factor behind the male lead character's demise and thus integral to the story line, never mind the fact that drugs were actually behind the King's own slow decline. Finally, and perhaps most stupidly, the Colonel insisted on a million dollars up front. Streisand countered by offering Elvis points on the film's back-end revenue, a deal structure that would have been far more lucrative in the long run than that million.

But the Colonel passed.

Streisand, despite her pitch to Elvis, was leery of the physical shape Elvis was in and suspect of his ability to get back down to camera-ready weight in time for filming. She was quick to count Elvis's pass on the film as a blessing and swiftly moved on to Kris Kristofferson for the part. The film was a mega hit. It won five Golden Globes, including Best Motion Picture and a Best Actor nab for Kristofferson. It won the Academy Award for Best Original Song and a Grammy Award for Best Album of Original Score for a Motion Picture.

Elvis was sunk. The film, had he done it, surely would have broken him out of the professional and personal rut he was in. Just as important, it would have allowed him to stretch out creatively, to express himself through something other than tired live Vegas revues. *A Star Is Born* would have made him relevant again.

But instead, he was barely relevant. In truth he was barely living. Awake but far from alive. The lost opportunity burned at him inside. He couldn't let the Streisand thing go. He demanded to speak to the Colonel. Alone.

Elvis stumbled into the adjacent room, shut the door, had a seat, dropped his head into his hands, and began talking. Quietly, politely but with passion and directness. He had something to say to the Colonel. Something he'd been holding back for some time. He ignored the gathering storm in his stomach and began:

"Colonel, you been good to me. For a long while. You done things for me that no one else coulda done, and for that I'm eternally grateful. But listen, you don't understand what *I* need. I don't think you understand where *I* need to be going. With my career. With my singing. With my acting. It's all Vegas this, Vegas that. Big auditoriums, coliseums, civic centers, and stadiums. But Colonel, I'm tired of that. Man, I've been playing for the back row for the past twenty years. I gotta hit 'em in the gut now. I gotta be making albums. Full artistic statements like that one Spector wanted to make with me. And no more cheesy movie soundtracks. And I need to be making films. No more lot-produced campy movies. Man, I shoulda done that second movie with Ann-Margret. You shoulda let me do that and you shoulda taken that offer from Streisand, man. I coulda killed in that role."

With that, the Colonel's famous temper made a predictable appearance. He snapped. The blowback was quick. Like it always was when they were behind closed doors.

"KILLED?!?! Killed what? Your career? How exactly would you have killed? As a drug-snorting has-been singer? What do you know about killing anyway?"

It was then that Elvis did something he'd never done before. He gave it back to the Colonel. Still seated, he pulled his head out of his hands, looked his manager in the eye, and let loose.

"Now you listen TO ME! I'm done. Done with the Cow Palace. Done with the Vegas revues. Done with the studio flicks and I'm done with you. That's it!"

The Colonel kept quiet for a second. Stared at his client. Collected himself as he endeavored to bury his temper and began to lay out his case.

"Elvis, what was I supposed to do? Let you record with Spector? Why? He needed you more than you needed him.

"Remember what you said back in '53 when you was getting

started? You said, 'I don't sound like nobody,' and you were right, and I took that to the bank and you made a lot of money because of it. You didn't need a producer or some high-handed songwriter to make you a star. You were bigger than the stars. Still are. You're Elvis."

He kept going. Starting to feel like he was beginning to get through to Elvis.

"So what? You want to be an *artist*? Why? You heard that record that Burton and Glen did with that country boy, Parsons. They called it a record, but a record of what exactly I don't know. Maybe it was a record of 'how *not* to have a hit' 'cuz there wasn't a-one on the entire thing.

"What is it, boy? What is it you want to do? You want to make pure country records like Jerry Lee does now? Why? He's playing one-night stands, even with radio at his back. I'm telling you, being an *artist* is a race to the bottom. You're bigger than that. You're your own thing. And I can sell *that thing*. I can't sell a heaping slab of 'listen to how interesting my goddamn feelings are.'"

The volume in the Colonel's voice started to increase. He caught himself, recalibrated his tone, and continued.

"Being an artist requires a lack of discipline. Artists are out there on the edge. Elvis, you of all people do not need less discipline. There is danger in a lack of discipline. You ain't capable of living high up on that wire. Look at you. You're barely capable of living down here with the rest of us. You're gonna what: Crawl into a studio for nine months with some overpriced producers and over-hyped songwriters and a big bag of your feelings? And for what? To come out the other side with something worth the people's time and money? Please. The records you been cutting have been making us money hand over fist since we started out. I know there ain't been a hit in a while, but you should look in the mirror to answer why that is. You ain't fit enough to go in for no studio work.

Not without a strict plan in place, and that's where I come in. I keep you on track."

Elvis slumped into himself. His body language indicating that as usual, he was coming around to the Colonel's way of thinking. The Colonel saw that he had his boy on the line and continued reeling him in, leaving just enough slack.

"You ain't no *artist*. You're an entertainer. If I'd let you chase that rabbit down that hole you woulda ended up like that Cooke fellow. Look at him. Tremendous entertainer. Mediocre artist at best, and what did he get for chasing his muse? Got himself shot to death in a two-dollar-a-night motel. Maybe he shoulda been working with the Colonel insteada Klein. I woulda kept him honest. Like I did you.

"All I'm saying is, why be something you ain't? You gonna chase the trends? What, you gonna cut your hair next and put safety pins in your clothes like them crazy kids EMI just dropped? You're better than that. You're an original. You don't need to shock and I'm telling you, that's where this business is going. In twenty years you're gonna have to wear your medicine on the outside just to get noticed. You're gonna have to either be crazy or just act crazy, 'cuz that's what the fans are gonna want—pure insanity. They're gonna demand that their rock stars act the fool 'cuz everything else will have been done by then. BUT YOU THE MAN WHO DONE IT FIRST! You broke the mold. You invented rock 'n' roll, boy! Not Bo Diddley. Not Chuck Berry, and sure as shit not Jerry Lee Lewis. You! Elvis Presley. You're the greatest entertainer of all time. You set the trends. You don't follow them. You know how many little wannabe Elvis Presley fans are born each day? They're gonna be recording new versions of 'Heartbreak Hotel' into the new millenium and long after both you and me are dead and in the ground."

Elvis took his head out of his hands. The Colonel's voice was still

The King and the beast within.

echoing but there was no Colonel in sight. Elvis felt his stomach roil. His legs were numb. He'd been sitting, in the same position, on his supermodern black toilet, in the bathroom adjacent to his master bedroom for too long. There was no Colonel in the room with him. Not in the flesh, anyway. This was a familiar version of a similar scene Elvis would play out in his head whenever he got his mind around to confronting the Colonel. Seldom did it advance to reality, a concept Elvis currently had no real grip on.

He sat, in agony, waiting for relief. He closed his eyes. Pushed. Nothing. When he opened them, what he saw sent fear bolting down his backbone. It was a reflection of himself. But not as he currently was, the overweight, speed-addled insomniac caught somewhere between delirium and delusion. Instead it was a reflection of his younger self, or perhaps just a version of his better self: svelte, perfectly styled hair, but wearing clothes Elvis never would have chosen. They were torn and frayed, second-hand-looking but perfectly fitted, casual, and thrown together. Denim jeans, ripped, patched, snug at the crotch, and tapered at the ankles with rolled cuffs. Black elevator boots with exposed steel toes. A cowboy shirt, tucked in with hand-stitched psychedelic designs, and mother-of-pearl snaps opened at the collar to expose the hair on his chest. A thick, black leather wristband and a white gold pinky ring. No belt. No need. The clothes fit that well. He was in perfect shape. Tall. Handsome beyond compare, just like he was in his youth but now with the added benefit of gravitas that only age and experience can suggest. His style was more bohemian than showbiz schmaltz, and cool in a way that Elvis couldn't quite figure out. And then there was the beard. Full. Nearing unkempt but with its wildness contrasted against an expertly coiffed pompadour; jet-black with a touch of gray slightly peppering the sides of his head. It all added up to an impossibly cool avatar of 1977 rock 'n' roll, a thinking man's Elvis brimming with sex appeal and fuck-all attitude. Southern charm by way of East Village cool: Skinny Elvis.

Fat Elvis knew this day would come. He knew that rumor was too ugly not to be true. The rumor that was whispered back in Tupelo during his youth. The rumor that followed him into adulthood on the lips of spiteful Southern music industry vets, the rumor that the Memphis Mafia all knew but dared not whisper, the rumor that Jerry Lee Lewis would tell to anyone who would listen, the rumor that that rock journalist in New York City was threatening to expose: The rumor that Elvis Presley's brother, Jesse Garon Presley, who had supposedly died at Elvis's side during birth, had actually lived and was given away by Elvis's parents to be raised by distant relatives in the hills of Mississippi because they were too poor to raise two children. Elvis always feared it was real. That his brother was alive and well. And that this day of reckoning would come.

Fat Elvis spoke with hesitation. "Jesse?"

Skinny Elvis was quick to reply, "You gotta be fucking kidding me, man. Jesse?" He mocked his overweight counterpart, "You stupider than I thought. *Jesse*. Shit. You believed them rumors? I ain't Jesse. I ain't your brother. C'mon. You *really* thinking all this time that your twin was alive? I can't believe you *actually* bought that jive."

Fat Elvis visibly cringed. Listening to someone, some*thing*, give voice to the shame he'd carried his whole life, it sent his blood pressure through the roof. Hearing it all out loud made it real. He was nervous. The pain in his stomach undeniable.

Skinny Elvis continued:

"Nah, man. I think you used that Jesse bullshit to hide from who you really were. Hide from what you were truly capable of. Your twin wasn't given away by your mama and Vernon to some hillbilly relatives up in Guntown. He's been dead for forty-two years."

Fat Elvis meets Skinny Elvis.

Fat Elvis sat, mouth agape. Caught between an epiphany and an epic breakdown.

Skinny Elvis pressed on. "The Colonel heard them rumors, too. That's right. He hung that shit over your head and you bought it. You jumped when he said jump because you was afraid he'd tell the world all about the Presleys and their dirty little secret: That your mama, Saint Gladys, and ol' boy Vernon gave Jesse away after he was born. Bullshit. Tupelo tabloid innuendo.

"The Colonel tried hanging it over your mama's head, too, and she was too afraid to confront him. Didn't want even the hint of a scandal out there. Afraid it woulda submarined your career before it got started. So she rode shotgun to your ambition, swallowed her pride, and let you sign on with the Colonel. The biggest mistake of her life. And yours, too.

"Problem was, you believed the *wrong* rumors, man. You believed that bullshit about Jesse when you shoulda given more account to the rumors about the Colonel."

Fat Elvis held focus on Skinny Elvis. Listening intently but unable to ignore his own envy. Skinny Elvis had all of his shit in one bag. He looked *incredible*. Fat Elvis couldn't believe those threads. They looked like rags spun into whatever the next generation of cool was going to wear. And his voice—his speaking voice—it had a command to it that Fat Elvis had completely lost. It had the air of an exotic down-home intellectual. Skinny Elvis spoke with the perfect mix of authority and empathy. He was listening to you, even while he was doing the talking. And he wasn't afraid to tell it like it was. He had some hair on him. The type of confidence that comes to only those who dare themselves to succeed. Fat Elvis watched and listened in awe as Skinny Elvis kept on with his monologue.

"'Colonel' Parker. He's about as much a 'colonel' as you is an 'actor.' That title is straight-up bullshit. The man ain't even *American*. You knew it, too, but you were too afraid to admit it. Ask yourself this, who loves money more than Colonel Tom Parker? No one! That's who. Promoters in Saudi Arabia offered you $5 million in cash for one show. The Colonel turned them down. Then they countered with $10 million and the Colonel turned them down again. He also turned down lucrative tours from promoters in Europe, South Africa, Asia…all at a time when frankly your outta-shape, uninspired, bordering-on-nonrelevant ass coulda used the money. Why? I'll tell you why: *Because he ain't got no passport.*

"He's an illegal. Tom Parker is a myth. Tom Parker was the name of the officer who enlisted a twenty-year-old Dutch carny barker named Andreas Cornelis van Kuijk into the U.S. Army in 1929 after his illegal entry into the United States."

Fat Elvis sat still on his toilet. Gripped.

Skinny Elvis continued: "It gets better. Or worse, depending. Andreas, now aka Tom Parker, went AWOL and was later, upon capture, diagnosed as psychotic. Yes sir. You been letting a legitimate psychopath manage your career all these years. Once he bounced out of the Army he took his carny talents to the music business and got his 'colonel' title off'a Governor Jimmie Davis for 'services rendered'—meanwhile his service record was a dishonorable discharge. That's right. That temper ain't no joke. Take that to the bank along with your 50 percent. Fifty percent!!!! Are you fucking kidding me, man? You're ELVIS PRESLEY! You gave that psycho half your money so he could lam it in style here in the States.

"That's right. Lam it. He's a bad, bad man. And not just for what he did to you. He might'a killed *your* spirit, but he might'a killed something else entirely back in the Netherlands."

Fat Elvis sat, transfixed, attempting to keep his face in an expression that said, *Tell me everything,* which was getting harder and harder for him to pull off while trying to simultaneously keep the pain in his gut at bay.

Skinny Elvis was undeterred. "He came here on the run, man.

Twenty years old and penniless. Just days after that girl died in the back of the grocer's store Andreas Cornelis van Kuijk worked at. Yards away from where Andreas lived. That girl was beaten. To death. By someone with a temper. She wouldn't give it up, either the money or the sex. No matter. She pissed someone off and that someone killed her. Ransacked the joint and doused the body with white pepper to throw the dogs off the scent. After it all went bad, Andreas vanished. Without a trace. Left no word with his family. Left everything behind. His money. His identification papers. His fancy clothing, including his expensive yellow topcoat that he was known to peacock around town in. He became a ghost. Split for the States. Penniless and alone and never once contacted his family again. Witnesses stated to police that the man seen entering the back of the grocer's store—the suspected killer—was a sharply dressed young man who wore a bright light yellow coat."

Fat Elvis's slack jaw fell into his lap.

"That's right. Light yellow; Colonel Tom Parker's favorite color."

Fat Elvis shook his head. He couldn't believe what he was hearing.

Skinny Elvis kept going. "Next thing you know, Andreas Cornelis van Kuijk is in the States enlisted in the Army as 'Tom Parker,' and the rest, as they say, is history. Tom Parker, the man you let manage your career and protect your interests. You know who he's really protecting? Himself, that's who. The art of it all ain't got nothing to do with it. Who's happier right now, man, you or Jerry Lee? Jerry Lee doesn't have them crowds no more but he's making the records he wants. He's tearing the ass outta them small rooms every night and raising hell with his band. Staying true to who he is. What are you doing except expanding your belt size? You're a far cry from what you coulda been because you were too afraid to risk it. Too afraid to confront the Colonel and your own past—blaming that bullshit on account of your brother might still be alive and the

Colonel might out the truth—but deep down you knew that wasn't the reason. What you were really afraid of was failing. You wanted to be an artist? My ass. Real artists take risks in the service of their art. They're free. Like me. Unafraid to expose themselves and brave enough to open themselves up to the criticism. Brave enough to corner that raging beast and to expose it through song. To set it free and to get down to who you really are. Even if it means cutting loose the one who brought you to the dance. You coulda dug in. Went for it. Done whatever the hell you wanted to do. Recorded your own damn version of *Ain't That Good News*. Written your own generation-defining version of "A Change Is Gonna Come" and exorcised all your demons in the process but you were too afraid, man."

Fat Elvis put his head in his hands. He was growing tired of the truth and weary of fighting off the immense pain in his gut. Nevertheless, Skinny Elvis persisted.

"But look at me, man. I'm you, motherfucker. I'm the real you."

His skinny counterpart did a quick karate chop to the hand-towel hanger on the wall. It was so precise that Fat Elvis burned with jealousy from his perch atop his toilet. Skinny Elvis looked at him with an expression that was part pride, part faux apology, as the brass hardware fell to the bathroom tile.

"I'm what you coulda been. The you that you were too afraid to become. I'm ten feet tall and been fresh outta fucks to give since I left the Louisiana Hayride. Fuck Bo Diddley. I'm just *forty-two* and I don't mind dying. I'm a real hunka hunka burnin' love. I get too close to myself and I catch hellfire 'cuz I'm hot, man. I ain't never needed no 'Comeback Special' 'cuz I ain't never been gone long enough to hafta come back. Ever since I got out of the Army, I gave up the ghost and told the Colonel we was through. Then I made the ALBUMS I wanted to make. Learned how to write my own songs. Worked with my own producers. I picked my own damn movies to act in and I acted the shit outta them. Motherfucker, I give *Brando* notes now. And he needs 'em 'cuz he's fatter than you. I took my shot and I hit it way outta the park. What did Chuck Berry say? 'Two–three count, nobody on. He hit a high fly into the stands.' Yeah, me too, and I'm rounded third and headed home 'cuz I'm *the* brown-eyed handsome man, motherfucker!"

Fat Elvis wasn't in awe and he wasn't amused. Now he was angry. His heart was racing. Rapidly pumping blood through his diseased arteries. Whatever was wrong with his stomach would no longer be ignored. Elvis bore down. Held his breath. Nothing moved. He shot Skinny Elvis a look that said, *Please…enough*, but Skinny Elvis kept going.

"Jerry Lee ain't the only killer. You killed somebody, too: me. This coulda been you. Look at me. I'm the greatest recording artist of all time. *And* the greatest entertainer. And the greatest songwriter. Greatest singer, too. I open my mouth to sing a song and the earth STOPS. Stevie Wonder calls ME for songwriting advice. I am the Beatles, the Rolling Stones, James Brown, Dean Martin, *and* Frank Sinatra rolled into one! Kris Kristofferson can't tune my guitar! You know why? 'Cuz I trapped that beast and I set him free. Maybe if you did the same thing you wouldn't'a been such an obsequious, pitiful, needy motherfucker. Look at you now. Fat. High. Strung out and miserable. You coulda been Skinny Elvis this whole time. You missed out, but you know what? It ain't too late. You can be Skinny Elvis forever now, man. You can be me. All you gotta do is give it up. Jesse's dead, man. Give up the ghost and grab that beast inside of you and let it go."

Fat Elvis, the King, was woozy sitting on his throne, the en suite toilet. He tried blocking out Skinny Elvis's voice, but his last words ran on a loop in Fat Elvis's head: *Give up the ghost and grab that beast inside of you and let it go.*

Elvis tried to do just that. He thought back as far as he could, playing the events of his life in reverse, tracked to the sound of Skinny Elvis's voice. He saw himself rewinding through two decades of fame and excess. The Colonel's image faded completely from his memory. Images of his father, Vernon, and his beloved mother, Gladys, became more and more clear in his mind's eye. Almost hyperreal. He tried remembering back to his infancy to grab an image of his brother. The one he'd always been able to imagine in life; his infant twin, happiness born in the flesh, but now—nothing. There was no image of Jesse, but that twin feeling of happiness was strong. Stronger than the guilt. Stronger than the fear and stronger than the grief ever had been. It overwhelmed him physically, it shortened his breath. He bore down, pushed one last time, and felt his heart *shudder* to a stop. He felt himself fall off the toilet and his face slam into the cold bathroom floor. Then the King felt nothing. Nothing but free.

ACKNOWLEDGMENTS

I never ever thought I'd write a book. Nobody did. Except my wife, Gabrielle. Without her constant belief in me, this book wouldn't have happened. And my sons, Harlan and Willem, who inspire me daily to get up and get after it; they need to be acknowledged, too. Maddie Caldwell, my editor, is directly responsible for this book being in your hands and for it being a way better book than it would have been without her vision. I'm grateful to Pat Healy for his writing assistance and ability to punch up phrases. I also benefited immensely from Pat's perspective on rock 'n' roll history and understanding of the characters and context within. Matt Nelson's amazing illustrations fueled me to create chapters worthy of their accompaniment. Somehow JD McPherson signified the words herein to my attention and I'm afraid of what might happen if I don't recognize that fact. Words are weird, Man. I would also like to acknowledge the loose group of folks who have supported and encouraged me throughout the writing of this book: the Nugents, the Vinczes, Oren Rosenbaum, Jamie Demas, Byrd Leavell, Sean Cahalin, Grace Royer, Callie Khouri, T-Bone Burnett, Michael Lohmann, Aaron Kaplan, Jake Shapiro, Conal Byrne, Dave Ambrose, Ellen Thibault, Ian Kennedy, Jared Gutstadt, Dennis Quaid, Brady Sadler, Mark Kates, Evan Kenney, Jay Cannava, Jackson Cannon, Dave Walsh, Dan Colby, Nick Palmacci, Taylor Bettinson, Carly Carioli, Chris O'Keeffe, Danny Poulin, Joe Sivick, Adam

Weiner, Chris Capotosto, Avi Spivak, Chris Wangro, Tom Perrotta, Eli "Paperboy" Reed, Aaron Mahnke, Steve Wilson, Lauren Osen, James Boggs, Chris Bannon, Scott Janovitz, Greg Conley, Will Dailey, David Ginsburg, Jon Lupfer, Ed Valauskas, Vernon Reid, Barry Tashian, Adam Taylor, Tony Goddess, Michael Creamer, Ryan Walsh, George Christie Jr., Jessie Rogers, Jen DiChiara, Jake Guralnick, Nick Lowe, Paul Q. Kolderie, Joe Gittleman, Phil Kaufman, Bob Pittman, Kirk Minihane, and Robert Christgau and Bob Dylan for agreeing with me.

BIBLIOGRAPHY

FAT ELVIS AND SKINNY ELVIS

My portrait of Elvis Presley was pulled into form from various sources. Chief among them, Peter Guralnick's *Last Train to Memphis* (Little, Brown, 1994) and HBO's excellent documentary on Elvis Presley from 2018 entitled, *The Searcher*, directed by Thom Zimny. Within that film, I found Tom Petty's thoughts on Colonel Parker and Elvis's artistry to be particularly compelling. Elvis's physical condition was sourced in part from a May 2, 2017, *Huffington Post* article by Garry Rodgers entitled "Elvis Presley's Death—What Really Happened to the King?" Skinny Elvis's riff on Andreas Corneilis van Kuijk's time in the Netherlands is sourced from Alanna Nash's book, *The Extraordinary Story of Colonel Tom Parker and Elvis Presley* (Simon & Schuster, 2001) as well as from the February 24, 2012, Smithsonianmag.com article by Mike Dash entitled, "Colonel Parker Managed Elvis' Career but Was He a Killer on the Lam?" The detailed cheese needed to describe Elvis's man cave, aka "the Jungle Room," came from reading the August 8, 2016, *Rolling Stone* article by Jordan Runtagh entitled, "Inside Elvis Presley's Legendary Man-Cave Studio" and from listening to RCA Records and Legacy Recordings' 2016 release of the Elvis Presley compilation of recordings, *Way Down in the Jungle Room*. Elvis was one king, but when it comes to writing about the hairy underbelly of American culture, Nick Tosches wears his own crown, and I am heavily indebted to him for his Esau Smith device from his excellent book, *Unsung Heroes of Rock 'n' Roll* (Da Capo Press, 1984), which inspired me to rethink the death and possible life of Jesse Garon Presley.

JERRY LEE LEWIS

I first read Richard Ben Cramer's article "The Strange and Mysterious Death of Mrs. Jerry Lee Lewis" when I was a boy. Probably fifteen years old. And it completely blew my mind. The idea that this rock 'n' roll icon, a man whose feet John Lennon kissed when he was inducted into the Rock 'n' Roll Hall of Fame, the idea that he could possibly be a killer and free and revered and oh yeah, his nickname is *The Killer!!!*——I just could not believe it. And the story never left me. I told everyone I could about it until eventually it inspired me to start a podcast. The article originally appeared in *Rolling Stone* on March 1, 1984, but I didn't catch up to it until much later when it appeared in a book of articles published by Rolling Stone. Of course, Nick Tosches's *Hellfire* (Grove Press, 1982) greatly influenced my depiction of Jerry Lee, as did Dennis Quaid's manic and inspired version of the Killer from the 1989 biopic *Great Balls of Fire*, directed by Jim McBride. Jim Sullivan's *Chicago Tribune* article from July 28, 1985, entitled, "Jerry Lee Lewis: The Killer Says the Wild Times Are Behind Him," and *People* magazine's "The Sudden Death of Wife No. 5 Confronts Jerry Lee Lewis with Tragedy—and Troubling Questions" from September 12, 1983, were also sources for this chapter.

DEAD, EURONYMOUS, AND VARG

Lords of Chaos (Feral House, 1998) by Michael Moynihan and Didrik Søderlind is *the* document on the rise of black metal or, as the authors put it, "the bloody rise of the satanic metal underground." It is essential reading for anyone interested in the topic. *Until the Light Takes Us* from 2008, directed by Aaron Aites and Audrey Ewell, was also critical in helping me gain insight into the feel of Norwegian black metal. An article from November 14, 2015, called "Norwegian Black Metal: Satanism, Church Burnings and Murder—What Hath Venom Wrought?" published on the *carwreckedbangs* blog, was instrumental in helping me piece together the history preceding the rise of black metal. The original *Kerrang* article, "Has Metal Gone Too Far?" by Jason Arnopp published March 27, 1993, was also a source for this chapter. And for a good dose of modern-day madness I would encourage anyone who was intrigued by this chapter to give Varg Vikernes's YouTube channel a spin. This wormhole went a long way in helping me understand Count Grishnackh.

GRAM PARSONS

For the Gram Parsons chapter, I heavily relied on *20,000 Roads: The Ballad of Gram Parsons and His Cosmic American Music* by David N. Meyer (Villard, 2007). In my opinion it is the most comprehensive take on Gram as both a person and as a musician. The passages on Gram's time with the Rolling Stones were particularly helpful, as was the *Guardian* article from April 24, 2010, by Sean O'Hagan entitled, "The Stones and the True Story of Exile on Main St." Details on the theft of Gram's body were sourced via the October 25, 1973, *Rolling Stone* article by Patrick Sullivan entitled, "Gram

Parsons: The Mysterious Death—and Aftermath," as well as the *Louder* article by Johnny Black entitled, "How I Stole Gram Parsons' Body," published on September 19, 2017. Bill Murray—always a north star—and his John Winger character from *Stripes*, directed by Ivan Reitman (1981), inspired the "dead before I'm thirty" bit. The incredibly talented Barry Tashian, who worked with Gram on his *GP* album, was super generous with his time in agreeing to talk to me about this part of Gram's creative life and personal life. Also, I was able to coax Phil Kaufman—the Mangler himself—to settle down long enough to jump on the phone with me, and the Gram chapter is better because of it.

AXL ROSE

There would likely be no Axl Rose chapter were it not for the book, *Watch You Bleed: The Saga of Guns N' Roses* (Gotham, 2008) by the legendary Stephen Davis. It provided a look into all corners of GNR's history and also into Axl's upbringing and psyche, and it was critical in helping me piece together this story. (Also, Stephen's book on Led Zeppelin, *Hammer of the Gods* [William Morrow, 1985] is about 70 percent responsible for my fascination with the music industry's dark history.) Daniel Durchholz's firsthand account of the Riverport Riot in the *Riverfront Times* from July 10, 1991, entitled, "Appetite for Destruction," as well as his article from July 26, 2017, in *Billboard* revisiting the event entitled, "Looking Back at the Riverport Riot as Guns N' Roses Return to St. Louis for First Show in 26 Years" were both crucial. Brandon Stosuy's December 12, 2008, *Stereogum* article, "Axl Rose on Chinese Democracy, Bipolarity, Running Late & Kanye West," and *Rolling Stone*'s "50 Wildest Guns N' Roses Moments" by Katherine Love, Wallace Morgan, Joseph Hudak, Keith Harris, Maura Johnston, and Dan Epstein were also sourced for his chapter as was *GQ's* January 13, 2016, article by Jeff Vrabel entitled, "Remember When Axl Rose Was Left Completely Unchecked During the Use Your Illusion Era?" Finally, Rob Tannenbaum's eye-opening *Rolling Stone* piece from November 17, 1988, the article that introduced us to Guns N' Roses entitled, "The Hard Truth About Guns N' Roses," was a blast to revisit and an important source in helping me understand the makeup of Axl Rose and his bandmates during their initial rise to rock dominance. Vernon Reid of Living Colour was cooler than my fifteen-year-old self could have hoped for and beyond generous in answering my questions about Axl's time in the media barrel after the "One in a Million" lyric controversy.

CHUCK BERRY

Chuck Berry is/was many things. Something he doesn't get enough credit for is his way with words. Too often we focus on his guitar playing, and for good reason, but that is at the expense of his other gift: writing. Chuck Berry, in my mind, is America's great poet. We hear the proof of that statement in his genre-defining early rock 'n' roll singles. But Chuck was also a great writer. Full stop. As I discovered in reading his book, *Chuck Berry: The Autobiography* (Harmony Books, 1987). At times the book is beautiful, enthralling, and sometimes damning (as you read in the quote I chose from the book at my chapter's end). Mike Sagar's "Sex, Drugs and Rock 'N' Roll Especially Sex," from the February 1993 issue of *Spy*, was a wild read and particularly compelling as a source. Other articles sourced for this chapter include: "The Story of Chuck Berry's 'Maybellene'" by Jesse Wegman, published by *NPR* (July 2, 2000); "The Chuck Berry I Knew" by Joe Edwards as told to Chad Garrison, published by *St. Louis Mag* (March 19, 2017); "Why Can't

We Be Honest About Chuck Berry?" by Andy Marino published by the *Outline* (March 20, 2017); "Chuck Berry Taped Women, Suit Charges" by Ralph Dummit, published by the *St. Louis Dispatch* (December 27, 1989); "The Perversions of Chuck Berry," from Bob Guccione's Archives, published by *VICE* (September 12, 2013); "Chuck Berry Was More Than a Rock Icon—He Was Also a Huge Pervert" by Bruce Golding for the *New York Post* (March 21, 2017). And finally, and perhaps most interesting of all, the September 1980 article from issue #7 of the local St. Louis punk rock 'zine, *Jet Lag* simply entitled, "Chuck Berry," where the father of rock 'n' roll himself, Chuck Berry, reviews records by the Sex Pistols, the Clash, and more. It was perhaps the most interesting piece of rock criticism I've ever encountered and was wholly responsible for creating a direct link between the Chuck Berry chapter and the Sid Vicious chapter.

SID VICIOUS

The Alan G. Parker–directed *Who Killed Nancy* from 2009 was particularly compelling, as was the *Telegraph*'s June 23, 2016, article by the *Telegraph* reporters entitled, "It Was Sid Vicious' Mum Who Gave Him Fatal Dose of Heroin Says Sex Pistols Photographer" for the Sid Vicious chapter. Additionally, Deborah Spungen's heartbreaking book about her daughter and Sid, *And I Don't Want to Live This Life* (Fawcett Crest, 1984) and Noel Monk's wild tour diary book, *12 Days on the Road* (Morrow, 1990) were crucial sources for this chapter. The following works were also informative in piecing together Sid's brief twenty-one years: the timeline on the website SidViciousLives.com; Thurston Moore's magical recounting of seeing Sid play at Max's Kansas City in *New York* magazine's "Greatest New York Ever: The Encyclopedia of Superlatives" (January 9,

2011); Charlotte Robinson's *PopMatters* article, "So Tough: The Boy Behind the Sid Vicious Myth" (June 14, 2006); "After 30 Years, a New Take on Sid, Nancy and a Punk Rock Mystery," written by Mark Brown and published by the *Guardian* on January 19, 2009; *The Filth and the Fury*, directed by Julien Temple (2000); *The Great Rock 'n' Roll Swindle*, also directed by Julien Temple (1980); Paul "Stan" Griffin's *Sid Vicious: Final 24—His Final Hours* (2008); as well as the multiple Sid and Nancy nodding-off clips on YouTube.

SAM COOKE

Once again Peter Guralnick's tremendous work *Dream Boogie: The Triumph of Sam Cooke* (Back Bay Books, 2005) was instrumental as a source for another one of my chapters. "Shooting of Sam Cooke Held 'Justifiable Homicide'" published in the *New York Times* on December 17, 1964, and "The Mysterious Death of Sam Cooke," written by Lydia Hutchinson and published in *Performing Songwriter* on December 11, 2016, were also used as sources for this chapter. Finally, perspective into Sam's death and insight into the postwar/ midcentury gospel scene was generously provided by the human soul encyclopedia, Eli "Paperboy" Reed.

LISA "LEFT EYE" LOPES

I fell in love with Lisa Lopes while writing about her in this chapter. Her badassery is rivaled only by Bertha Lee Franklin from the previous chapter on Sam Cooke, and it is all on display in VH1 RockDocs' *The Last Days of Left Eye* from 2007, which was the main source for this chapter. Additionally *Rolling Stone*'s "Life of Fiery Rapper Lisa Lopes Tragically Cut Short" by David

Keeps, published on June 6, 2002; and "Lisa Lopes, Rapper, Dies in Honduras Crash at 30" by Jon Pareles, from the April 27, 2002, issue of the *New York Times*.

PHIL SPECTOR

Phil Spector has inspired countless think pieces, documentaries, and biographies. These, along with his many interviews over the years, provided a treasure trove of information to piece together this chapter with. The quote attributed from Phil to John Lennon's ghost about Elvis Presley was taken from the *Rolling Stone* interview Phil did with Jann Wenner from the November 1, 1969, issue. The interview is one of the wildest things I've ever read, and I highly recommend you dig it up. *True Crime with Aphrodite Jones: Phil Spector* (2010); *Tearing Down the Wall of Sound: The Rise and Fall of Phil Spector* by Mick Brown (Knopf, 2007); the HBO film *Phil Spector*, written and directed by David Mamet (2013); *Be My Baby: How I Survived Mascara, Miniskirts and Madness...* by Ronnie Spector (Harmony, 1990); *The Lives of John Lennon* by Albert Goldman (William Morrow, 1988); "Phil Spector's Cheap Shots" by Dominick Dunne, published in *Vanity Fair* in October 2007; and the *MentalFloss* article "5 Artists Reportedly Held at Gunpoint by Phil Spector" by Bill Demain, published August 1, 2001, were all sourced for this chapter.

INDEX

ABOUT THE AUTHOR

Jake Brennan is the writer, host, and producer of *Disgraceland*, a rock 'n' roll true crime podcast, which exploded onto the scene in 2018. Jake saw his dad's band open for the Ramones when he was ten years old. Before the show he asked his dad what the Ramones sounded like. He was told, "They sound like The Beach Boys but louder and faster." Later that night, Jake learned that his dad was right. He also learned the importance of history in understanding music. Since then, Jake has been obsessed with music. And history. And for whatever reason, the darker sides of both. *Disgraceland* combines these obsessions. Jake lives north of Boston with his wife and two sons. He is surrounded by history and surrounds himself with music. Sometimes it's louder and sometimes it's faster, but it's never as cool as the Ramones.